THE DIFFERENCE HEAVEN MAKES

THE DIFFERENCE HEAVEN MAKES

Rehearing the Gospel As News

Christopher Morse

t&t clark

Published by T&T Clark International
A *Continuum Imprint*
The Tower Building, 11 York Road, London SE1 7NX
80 Maiden Lane, Suite 704, New York, NY 10038

www.continuumbooks.com

British Library Cataloguing-in-Publication Data
A catalogue record for this book is available from the British Library

ISBN: 978-0-567-42524-9 (Hardback)
         978-0-567-02733-7 (Paperback)

Typeset by Pindar NZ, Auckland, New Zealand
Printed and bound in the United States of America

To the many students and other friends in the academy, the churches, and elsewhere who have been "sharers of the Gospel" with me in the thinking of these pages.

CONTENTS

—— ❖ ——

PREFACE

It was a cold Maine morning, minus eight degrees Fahrenheit, when I arrived at Bangor Theological Seminary, now more than a decade ago, to deliver what was billed as a convocation address on heaven. Along with the compensating warmth of my hosts' gracious welcome, the additional chill of one unexpected response from the floor when I had concluded has remained with me ever since. In a tone more of disappointment than of censure an individual came to the microphone and said, "I have listened to everything you had to say, and you never got to the subject!"

Getting to the subject of heaven as we hear of it in the testimony called the Gospel, and how it may be said to matter as purportedly the best news anyone could ever hear, has proved more demanding, but also far more intriguing, than I had initially realized. I have found myself coming back to it at every available opportunity with a growing realization of how much was at stake.

The premise addressed in the reflections of these pages is that references to heaven in the Bible have more present day significance than is routinely associated with the word today. Navigating the range of this current significance to its contextual source presents a fascinating task. No subject more than this news of "heaven" so resists attempts by definers of the modern mind to foreclose consideration of what living in the real world involves. How this hearing of "a species beyond," in the words of the poet Emily Dickinson, both "beckons and baffles" reopens one of the most important theological legacies of the past century and respectfully asks of it, "So what?"

Where I have made earlier forays into various aspects of this subject, or spelled out this distillation in more detail, I have provided endnotes, but I have deliberately sought to remain focused upon the title and thereby keep the bibliographical endnotes to an essential minimum.

My gratitude is extended as always to the students at Union in the several seminars where some of the issues and individual theologians that appear here were studied, and to other scholarly colleagues as well, J. Louis Martyn, Dorothy Martyn, James F. Kay, Therese DeLisio, Trevor Eppehimer, and Marianne LaFrance, who responded to portions of the manuscript at its various stages. For first suggesting the cover painting and photographing it I am indebted to Candace Goetz, and to Robert Weatherford, the artist, I offer my most sincere thanks for the permission to use it. My thanks go also to Kent A. Reynolds for his expertise in the biblical languages, to Burke Gerstenschläger, who as the initial editor facilitated this project, to Justin Lasser, now completing his doctorate, for his assistance in copy-editing the final text, and to Thomas Kraft, Katie Gallof, and all their associates at T&T Clark who brought its publication to completion.

Further, my deep appreciation is expressed to the local churches and pastors' schools that have engaged with me on this topic and for the opportunities to deliver lectures or papers on some of the developing aspects of it at the American Theological Society, the Duodecim Theological Society, the New Haven Theological Discussion Group, Bangor Theological Seminary, Wesley Theological Seminary, The Seminary of the West Indies in Kingston, Jamaica, Drake University, and the Scottish Universities of Aberdeen, St. Andrews, Edinburgh, and Glasgow.

During the years of my concentration on this subject Craig Berggren has encouraged my efforts by taking time to read, re-read, listen to, and critically discuss each chapter in its preparation. His is an essential friendship, best expressed for me by Paul's words in Philippians 1.3.

Chapter 1

HEARING OF HEAVEN TODAY

One need not be a member of any particular community of faith to be interested in the subject of heaven. But what the subject of heaven is varies with particular communities, including the more secular community of our everyday English speech. We have all heard the word "heaven" and commonly associate certain ideas with it. We may think of it in terms of the sky, life after death, or a state of bliss. We may say that we believe in heaven, or that we do not. The aim in these pages is not to impose a single hearing of the word as the only one. How heaven may sound to us cannot be legislated. Nor is it to look for points of similarity among various traditions. Prevalence of belief or unbelief is not the issue. Rather, it is to ask a question that any community, or individual within it, is free to ask; namely, what follows if we hear of heaven in *this* particular way? The way considered in these pages is that of attending to references to heaven in what the Christian church listens to as news it calls good, the Gospel. In what sense do these references when heard in their context make sense? It is this particular context of usage that will here provide the focus for inquiring into the difference our hearing of heaven makes. To participate in communities of Christian faith is to engage in talk of heaven. Less evident is what we are hearing and saying when we do so. To those who grow up in the church the talk of heaven comes early: "Our Father, who art in heaven, hallowed be Thy name. Thy kingdom come, Thy will be done on earth as it is in heaven." The questions come later, if they do. Growing up is to become accountable for our words, to clarify what we do *not* mean, even when sometimes we are not sure what we do mean. Hearing of heaven today calls for such accountability.

In 1941 one of the most influential New Testament scholars of the time, Rudolf Bultmann, wrote that "there is no longer any heaven in the old (*alten*) sense of the word."[1] Yet a Bible today with all references to "heaven" blotted out, we must admit, would look like a very censored document indeed. Depending upon the English version cited, and its translation of the Hebrew *šāmayim* (שָׁמַיִם) and the Greek *ouranos* (οὐρανός), there are about six hundred and seventy-five appearances of the words "heaven" or "the heavens" in the Old and New Testaments. Few of our currently more emphasized theological subjects in comparison can claim to be mentioned in these scriptures as often.

Furthermore, the language most Christians speak today as a church, whether absent-mindedly or not, is full of this ancient vocabulary of heaven. The God who is prayed to as "Our Father in heaven" is affirmed in the creeds as "Maker of heaven and earth," whose Word enfleshed in Jesus Christ "for us humans and for our salvation came down from heaven," proclaiming news that "the kingdom of heaven is at hand." This Jesus, so we read and hear preached, taught in parables about the coming of heaven, saying "the kingdom of heaven is like this," then crucified and risen "ascended into heaven," and is confessed as the One who shall come "from thence . . . to judge the living and the dead." With news of God's life-giving Holy Spirit descending from heaven, a threefold reference to God's grace as a triunity is ever praised, so the church sings, "with all the company of heaven."

How, if at all, may the hearing of such references to heaven be said to matter today? Certainly Bultmann was correct in writing that, from the standpoint of modern science and cosmology, our notions of space are very different from primitive ideas of a three-tiered universe, with heaven up in the sky, hell down under the ground, and a flat earth in between. In that ancient, cosmological sense of the word there is no longer any heaven. We may still speak of the skies as the heavens, but unlike earlier ages it adds nothing to our natural science to do so. Whatever we may say, we do not negotiate our way in this physical universe in reference to a three-storied cosmology of heaven above, and hell below, with a flat earth in between. And every time we step onto a plane, whether we consider ourselves fundamentalists or liberals, we show that we share this modern mind-set. All critically educated students of the New Testament from the time of Rudolf Bultmann are aware of his influence and are indebted to the questions concerning heaven that his work poses.

Whether we regard the earliest inscriptions on the Egyptian pyramid walls that date from the third millennium before the birth of Jesus, or consider the Ptolemaic astronomy that informs Dante's medieval account of *Paradiso* at the beginning of the fourteenth century, it is obvious that these depictions of heaven assume worldviews outside the frame of reference of theories of matter and anti-matter in today's astrophysics. As far as scientific cosmology is at issue — or what some textbooks in modern astronomy still curiously refer to as "celestial mechanics" — the celestial in the old sense of the word is indeed no more. In this regard Bultmann rightly speaks for a consensus in the critical New Testament scholarship of the twentieth century. Students of the Gospel have been taught to distinguish between the *kernel* of its enduring message and the mythological *husks* of the outdated worldviews by which, in pre-scientific times, this message was initially expressed. Often considered, however, to be among these dispensable husks or mere wrappings are the Bible's references to heaven. This presumptive disposal of heaven as husk forecloses any further hearing of the difference that heaven makes. That is the crucial issue this influential twentieth century legacy now poses for us today.

Heaven as Commonly Referred to

We in the church have no monopoly, of course, on talk of heaven, or of things celestial. Three centuries prior to the time of Jesus, Aristotle, as well as Plato before him, wrote of the heavens in a treatise still studied by philosophers today. From the Greek term for heaven, *ouranos*, we get the name for the planet *Uranus. Ouranos*, Aristotle writes, is the ultimate periphery of all things, "the outermost region in particular . . . in which we say that everything divine has its seat as well."[2] To speak of the heavens, in Aristotle's view, is to speak of the cosmos. This outermost region of the heavens is said to be distinguished from the four elements of earth, air, fire, and water by an everlasting ether (αἰθέρα) that constantly circles overhead.[3] Aristotle's cosmology is consistent with his theology, with his understanding of the divine.

To hear what Aristotle has to say cosmologically about heaven is to think of the sky, that upper ethereal sphere of which the ancients wrote that overarches the earth. Parallels can be drawn from many traditions of antiquity, including the traditions of Genesis, and of elsewhere in the Bible as well. Heaven, in this first instance, within this cosmological frame of reference, is taken to refer to that which is up above, as distinguished from that which is here on earth. Here the contrasting terms are "heaven" and "earth."

I suspect, however, that what most likely comes to mind when we hear the word "heaven," in any serious sense, is not so much the sky, but life after death. This fact is illustrated by the hybrid terms we have devised to refer to heaven as an "afterlife," "the hereafter," or even, "the sweet by and by." This association also is rooted in antiquity, for it is a common thought that immortality is found the higher the ascent from earth. "Participating in eternity," is the way Saint Augustine characterized the highest heaven.[4] Dante wrote of the souls of the blessed ascending to the tenth heaven of Paradise, propelled as an arrow from a bow upwards toward "the Love that moves the sun and the other stars."[5] In this second instance, heaven is taken to mean the good place above where we go when we die, distinguished from hell, the inferno below, the bad place. Here the contrasting terms are "heaven" and "hell."

Historical accounts support the claim that ancient usage associates heaven, or the heavens, with the sky and contrasts heaven with the earth. It also associates heaven with a blessed life of bliss after death and contrasts heaven with hell, a doomed hereafter. Instances of this usage may be found in the Bible. And we today in casual conversation still describe our most blissful pleasures as "heavenly." Modern studies of the history of images of heaven have concentrated on one or more of these familiar associations: defining heaven as an "upperworld,"[6] or as "what happens after death,"[7] or a "state of being,"[8] or "fulfillment of . . . human longing."[9] These informative works offer descriptive accounts of comparative depictions and myths reflective of the spirit of their times. They do not, by design, address the theological task of testing the spirits in order to assess what constitutes a faithful hearing of heaven, and what does not, in keeping with the news of the Gospel. This testing is the task of dogmatics.[10]

Uncommon References to Heaven

Contrary to a *Time* magazine cover portraying a fluffy cloud bearing a man peering out into an all blue yonder with the byline, "Does heaven exist?,"[11] most of the references to "heaven" in the Gospel testimony are not about blue skies or life only after death. Remarkably few of the approximately six hundred and seventy-five instances of the term found in the Bible may be said to be reducible to such categories of interpretation. In such testimony, heaven neither begins nor ends with death. The automatic tendency to suppose when we hear the word "heaven" that the subject is either the sky or the hereafter only shows how much our own thinking has become conformed to the world of the *Time* magazine cover. The question is, *what* "sense of the word" do we have in mind when we hear of heaven?

At the outset, at least, this much seems clear. Those of us who are part of the church are regularly hearing in our scriptures, hymns, creeds, and prayers, mention of heaven. And what Bultmann called "the old sense of the word" is not the only sense in which this testimony is subject to being heard today. In fact, if the term "*post*modernism" means anything at all, it is that there is more present-day significance in traditions of discourse than can be limited simply to one controlling sense either of an old, or of a so-called modern, worldview.

In the news called the Gospel we encounter a less conventional usage. Given ears to hear, it almost sounds as if a different subject than what we ordinarily suppose is being talked about.

To anticipate, the heaven heard of in the context of this so-called "good news" (εὐαγγέλιον, *evangel*) is less about a place we go to than one that comes to us, less about a postmortem afterlife than about life here and now, and less about a timeless, static state than about a timely taking-place. Yet, in this hearing, heaven is also not reducible simply to psychological terms, a feeling of bliss, or a form of consciousness allegedly alterable by spiritual practices or techniques. It is not the word, but the frame of reference, that determines what the subject of heaven is.

While the range of significance in this language of the biblical scriptures and the worship of the church is not condensable solely to a single concept or uniform view, "heaven" in this context of usage is most characteristically associated with news of *life* that is said to be *now coming toward us*. This confessed "life of the world to come," as the fourth-century Nicene Creed affirms it, extends, to be sure, beyond our earthly death, but its coming is said to be an arriving kingdom, or *basileia*, from heaven "at hand" on this earth. This *basileia*, as it is variously announced in the Gospel writings, is not limited to what we tend to call "a state of mind," though that is said to be involved. It sounds more encompassing, like a state of affairs taking shape. The church's prayer is that this "kingdom come" and that the will of heaven this day "be done on earth as it is in heaven." Here indeed is a most unconventional sense of purportedly the real world as that which is now *at hand* in the coming of heaven.

In this third instance, "heaven," with respect to this coming state of affairs, is contrasted neither with the earth, nor with hell as a hereafter, but with what the Apostle Paul denotes as "the form (σχῆμα, *schema*) of this world [that] is passing away" (1 Cor. 7.31). What we now hear of heaven, and even find ourselves confessing in the worship of the church, is that heaven comes to earth, and even to the depths of hell. "He descended into hell (*ad inferna* or *ad inferos*)," so the Apostles' Creed affirms of the One proclaimed as "descended from heaven" (Jn 3.13).[12] This is not at all the way heaven is conventionally spoken of. The contrast, in this third instance, is drawn between heaven as what is coming to pass, in the sense of taking place, as distinguished from what is said to be passing away.[13] This introduces a new way of associating the first two instances of the more commonly linked terms "heaven and earth" and "heaven and hell."

Consider then a thought experiment: *If we take this third way of hearing of heaven — namely, heaven as "that which is now at hand and coming to pass" contrasted to "that which is passing away" — as the Gospel's primary frame of reference for hearing what is said of "heaven and earth" and "heaven and hell," what would the implications be? How much would it matter in considering and facing what we call "the real world"?*

Heaven's Coming to Pass

Central to the message of the Gospel is news that a *basileia* (βασιλεία) from heaven is "at hand" (ἐγγύς). What the original Greek term *basileia* in the context of the Gospel testimony conveys is a sense of a dominion, and it is usually translated into English as "kingdom," or "reign," or "realm." To avoid imperialistic connotations, the word "commonwealth" has also come to be favored. (As one who grew up in Virginia, the combined terms of "The Commonwealth of the Old Dominion" are not unfamiliar!) But it is a dominion that is now said to be coming to pass and *taking place* in our midst. It is not a dominion, or state of affairs, that is already *in place* as part of the form of this world that is passing away. In short, this *basileia* is announced as *at* hand, but not as *in* hand.

The more common expression is "the *basileia* of God," an expression found throughout the New Testament, but primarily in some fifty-one references in the Gospels of Matthew, Mark, and Luke. While it is true that only Matthew, in twenty-eight additional instances, uses the explicit term "the *basileia* of heaven," the coming of this *basileia* of God is consistently said throughout the New Testament to be a coming that is *from* heaven. This reflects the prevailing usage of the Bible, where that which comes from God is most characteristically described as coming from heaven. To dismiss this usage as outdated and no longer of consequence in the twenty-first century is to disregard the question of a text's context. The *locus*, so to speak, of all of God's dealings in this textual context is heaven. But the *focus* of all of heaven's dealings is earth. What we are told of the *basileia* is that it both comes from heaven and is now at hand. Similarly, Paul refers to the expected Lord's coming from heaven, in writing to the Philippians, with the words, "The Lord is at hand" (Phil. 4.5). Again, to the Romans his words are that "the day is at hand" (Rom. 13.12). So also the author of James writes that "the coming of the Lord is at hand" (James 5.8). It is this announced at-handedness of heaven's coming that most calls into question our conventional assumptions of what the subject of heaven is about. By being confronted with this term "at hand" (ἐγγύς), Christian theology today is presented with some of its most intriguing issues.

For those who are interested today in the subject of heaven, a rehearing then would seem to be called for. I emphasize the words "hearing" and "rehearing" quite deliberately for several reasons that I think are pertinent to the proposed thought experiment. The sixteenth-century reformer John Calvin aptly observed that not all to whom the Gospel, or in his words "covenant of life," is preached hear it as such, and that the church exists wherever the Word of God is not only purely preached and the sacraments rightly administered, but where this proclaimed Word is "heard" (*audiri*, audited).[14] This is reflective of the Apostle Paul's understanding, before there was a written New Testament as we know it, that faith comes by hearing that which is spoken of Christ (Rom. 10.16). Also the Letter to the Hebrews calls for "greater attention to what we have heard" (Heb. 2.1).

If the Gospel (εὐαγγέλιον) is really to be heard as news, as the Greek components of its name "Good (εὐ) News (ἀγγελία)" would appear to indicate, then its hearing must be said in some respect to contain something new.[15] That hearing news involves hearing something new may seem an obvious point, but it is crucial. News is not history. It makes history, and may become history, as our expression "news event" suggests. One context of news reporting is its historical context, in the sense of the setting in which it may have originated. But whether what is reported as news is heard as such is not subject to determination by methods of historical research in the way that the reports themselves are. This is the difference between a hearing of the Gospel as news and a reading of the Gospel as a set of texts native only to an earlier time. To limit the significance of the Gospel references to heaven to their ancient setting, or historical context of origin, would be to take them out of the context of news. We must bear this in mind when we speak of hearing the Gospel references in their proper context.

Furthermore, terms such as "hearing" and "rehearing" carry a dual meaning. Any hearing, by definition, involves listening as the detecting of sounds. But it is instructive that we also use the word "hearing" in the sense of a weighing of testimony, or a courtroom trial. To hold a hearing of testimony in a judicial proceeding is spoken of as trying a case. In like manner, we may use the word "auditing" to mean both a listening, as in auditing a lecture, and an accounting, as in a taking of inventory. In proposing that a rehearing of the Gospel testimony regarding heaven is called for today, both the sense of a new trying of the evidence, or new accounting, as well as the sense of a new listening are intended. Here the question of the trustworthiness of the news report arises. More will be said of this accountability as a task of theology in Chapter 2.

Some Soundings

By referring to "the Gospel talk," or "the Gospel testimony," I mean the news that the New Testament depicts as entrusted and commissioned, but not restricted, to the followers of Jesus Christ. This news is conveyed by what the church comes to call the Old Testament, as well as the New. It is not limited only to the first four books of the New Testament, explicitly called the Gospels According to Matthew, Mark, Luke, and John. Paul reminds the Corinthians of "the gospel that I proclaimed to you," literally, "the gospel that I gospeled to you" (1 Cor. 15.1). A similar theme appears in his other epistles as well, as it does in most of the writings of the New Testament. The Johannine texts characteristically use the term "word" rather than "gospel," but in doing so they also speak, as in the First Letter of John, of "news" (ἀγγελία) "that we have heard" and "proclaim"(1 Jn 1.5).

But this Gospel talk is only heard as *God's* good news, whatever its textual origin or genre, when it attests itself as such to its followers. Only then does it become for its hearers a contemporary news event. An announcement that is not heard is not news, either good or bad. As a news event, the Gospel references to heaven are taken not as fragmented texts in isolation having no bearing upon one another, but as a coherent message that calls forth a current following. This following the New Testament denotes simply as "those called forth" (the ἐκκλησία, or in Latin, *ecclesia*), the New Testament word translated in English as "church."

Precisely because of its reception as news of heaven the impact of this particular talk cannot be predetermined by its earthly announcers. What is heard is not subject to human production, nor can it be imposed by any scholarly or ecclesial controls — a most remarkable state of affairs, if one thinks about it, that has historically confounded all who presume to exercise a custodianship of this news, whether from the church or the academy. Rather, the scribe trained for the *basileia* of heaven, we are told, is "like a householder who brings out of his treasure what is new and what is old" (Mt. 13.52). Any following of the sound of this news "about heavenly things" (Jn 3.12), according to Jesus' reported dialogue with Nicodemus, is more comparable to the blowing of the wind. "The wind blows where it chooses, and you hear the sound of it, but you do not know where it comes from or where it goes" (Jn 3.8). "Pay attention to what you hear," are the recounted words of Jesus to the disciples (Mk 4.24, Lk. 8.18). Within this particular context of usage whatever we may profess to know of heaven is more accurately characterized as a knowledge of soundings, of how the Gospel testimonies regarding heaven may be said to resound, rather than as a knowledge of established or establishable facts.

Lines from the poet Emily Dickinson characterize that which stands beyond this world as invisible, "but positive, as Sound." Without presuming to claim Dickinson's agreement with the content of these pages, I find in the imagery of her exacting poetic brevity an apt touchstone around which a number of points that emerge for consideration from the Gospel references to heaven may be said to coalesce.[16]

> This World is not Conclusion.
> A Species stands beyond —
> Invisible, as Music —
> But positive, as Sound —
> It beckons, and it baffles —
> Philosophy — don't know —
> And through a Riddle, at the last —
> Sagacity, must go —
> To guess it, puzzles scholars —
> To gain it, Men have borne
> Contempt of Generations
> And Crucifixion, shown —
> Faith slips — and laughs, and rallies —
> Blushes, if any see —
> Plucks at a twig of Evidence —
> And asks a Vane, the way —
> Much Gesture, from the Pulpit —
> Strong Hallelujahs roll —
> Narcotics cannot still the Tooth
> That nibbles at the soul —

Listening again to the biblical traditions of gospeling we may detect today four recurring sounds of heaven, or of what Dickinson calls "the Species beyond" this world's inconclusiveness, that beckon and baffle most prominently. These are interrelated but distinguishable. They have to do with heaven (1) as the course of God's forthcoming, (2) as created, (3) as a community, and (4) as, so we have noted, a *basileia* at hand.

1. *Heaven as the Course of God's Forthcoming*

References to heaven as God's dwelling place emphasize not a state of confinement but the direction from which God is said to act in relation to the earth. Thus, it is more consistent with this usage to hear of the locus and focus of heaven as the directional course of God's forthcoming toward earth. Testimony from the book of 1 Kings illustrates the point. Here heaven is referred to in prayer to the Lord God as "your dwelling place." But this dwelling is explicitly acknowledged to be no container of God: "Even heaven and the highest heaven cannot contain you . . ." (1 Kings 8.27).[17] Rather, God is invoked to "hear in heaven your dwelling place, and do according to all that the foreigner calls to you, so that all the peoples of the earth may know your name and fear you . . ." (1 Kings 8.43). The heavenly dwelling place is depicted as the place of God's *doing* for all the peoples of the earth. It is God's course of action. The leitmotiv of "hear in heaven and do on earth" runs throughout scriptural prayers of petition to God.

Whatever comes from God is said to come from heaven. From this direction in relation to earth, God hears, speaks, and acts. Manna is provided in the wilderness as "bread from heaven" (Exod. 16.4). Regarding this manna, the words of Jesus to his disciples in the Gospel of John are that "the bread of heaven is that which comes down from heaven and gives life to the world" (Jn 6.33). This bread of life from heaven is characterized as neither stale nor preservable. The Israelites in the wilderness do not receive it ahead of time or before its time. Nor can they keep it after its time (Exod. 16.4). We hear of this bread of heaven only as "our daily bread" (Mt. 6.11). Most basic to all of the sounds of the Gospel is this association of heaven with life that is currently coming to meet us. Whatever sense it may make, it is certainly news to hear that our life is daily a fresh occurrence of heaven.

At the same time, attention to the Gospel message of God's directional forthcoming counters any attempts to equate this fresh occurrence of heaven with some euphoria of raised consciousness or an induced emotional bliss. This is so because what is said to come from heaven are not only showers of blessings but also the thunder and storm clouds of judgment. More exactly, the mercies from heaven are themselves heard to include the taking place of God's righteous judgment. God's wrath is revealed from heaven (Rom. 1.18). From the Psalms we hear that the Lord who "rained down" on Israel "manna to eat and gave them the grain of heaven" (Ps. 78.24) also "uttered judgment" from heaven "to save all the oppressed of the earth" (Ps. 76.8-9). No religious practices or spiritual techniques produce heaven in this sense.

Most especially, what is said in the Gospel accounts to happen in the full life-span depicted of Jesus Christ from preexistence through the events of the Cross to the Parousia, or Second Coming, happens in relation to heaven. God's forthcoming from heaven is presented in the passion, crucifixion, and descent into hell, no less than in the annunciation, nativity, baptism by John, earthly ministry, resurrection, and ascension. Each dimension of the span of Jesus' life as gospeled, beginning with the Word that "was with God" and that "was God" (Jn 1.1), is recounted with particular reference to some aspect of God's forthcoming from heaven, whether it be God's promise, voice, or power, portrayed in terms of giving, sending, judging, healing, raising, and the hearing of prayer. "For I have come down from heaven," so we hear in John's Gospel, "not to do my own will, but the will of him who sent me" (Jn 6.38). It is thus only the One crucified who is hereby heard of as risen, and awaited as coming from heaven in final judgment and glory to all the living and the dead. Whatever we hear praised as the beauty and glory of heaven, according to how the course of God's forthcoming sounds in this particular Gospel testimony, is praised only by taking account of the deepest sufferings and betrayals of earth. "No one has ascended into heaven except the one," and all this one encompasses, "who descended from heaven, the Son of Man" (Jn 3.13). What happens on earth is inseparable from the course heaven takes. As heard in a hymn of the church regarding the ascension into heaven of the crucified Christ, it is precisely "those wounds, yet visible above," that are "in beauty glorified."[18] In such a hearing the wounds of earth to the depths of hell are not rendered invisible by the beauty and glory of heaven. Once again, whatever sense it may make, it is news, baffling at least initially for some of us, to hear that heaven is no state of denial of the harshest realities of earth. Nor is heaven any feel-good narcotic available for religious marketing, Dickinson's "Much Gesture, from the Pulpit," or what Dietrich Bonhoeffer famously called "cheap grace."[19]

    This first sound of heaven as the course of God's action directed toward earth enables us to hear of Jesus "looking up to heaven" (Mt. 14.19) and being "taken up to heaven" (Acts 1.2) in other than only spatial terms. Talk of ascent, as well as descent, may employ spatial imagery. But a world of difference exists between hearing that Jesus looks skyward, and is taken up into the sky, and in hearing that Jesus looks to, and is taken up into, the very life that is now forthcoming toward us. This rehearing is especially significant when we bear in mind that the Jesus of the Gospel message is identified with "the way, the truth, and the life" (Jn 14.6). The news is that it is this way, and truth, and life of heaven that is currently coming to pass, and not passing away, in our midst. Thus the ascension account in Acts that tells of the disciples "gazing up toward heaven" as Jesus is lifted up into a cloud concludes with a question said to be posed by two men in white robes suddenly standing nearby who ask, "Men of Galilee, why do you stand looking up toward heaven? This Jesus, who has been taken up from you into heaven will come in the same way as you saw him go into heaven" (Acts 1.10-11). Here the direction of heaven in relation to the disciples is depicted not as their looking up above the earth, or overlooking the earth, but as looking ahead or forward to what is promised to come into the very situation that now faces the disciples where they are on earth. So they returned to the city, we hear, where, at the day of Pentecost, "suddenly from heaven there came a sound like the rush of an overpowering wind" (Acts 2.1). At this sound "devout Jews from every nation under heaven living in Jerusalem" heard the disciples speak of God's mighty acts in language that they could understand (Acts 2.1-13). "They were amazed and perplexed," the account tells us, by the sound of heaven coming to them (Acts 2.12). "It beckons, and it baffles," are Emily Dickinson's words.

Likewise, in yet another account given in Ephesians of the raising of Jesus to God's "right hand in the heavenly places" no spatial metaphors are even employed. Rather, Jesus' position in heaven is described, not as far above the ground, but as "far above all rule and authority and power and dominion, and above every name that is named, not only in this age but also in the age to come" (Eph. 1.21). Those addressed by this letter are even told that they themselves have been raised with Christ and now "sit with him in the heavenly places" (Eph. 2.6). Most extraordinary of all, and what can only be news to most hearers to whom Ephesians speaks, is the word that precisely because they now are "seated" in heaven with Christ they are enabled to "walk" here and now worthily with one another in the affairs of earth "making the most of the time" and to "wrestle" without being defeated in contention with all the principalities and powers that are currently seeking to rule the present world in darkness (Eph. 5.15-16, 6.12). Where they are "seated" in heaven is said to be what enables them to "stand" and "wrestle" on earth (Eph. 6.12-14), a message that surely gives new meaning today to the political adage that where one stands on any issue depends upon where one sits, or has one's power base and social location.

A further reference that sounds strikingly different when heaven is heard as the course of God's forthcoming and not only as the sky, the hereafter, or a feeling of bliss, is the confession of having "sinned against heaven." The younger brother in Luke's account, who is said to come to himself after squandering his inheritance in a distant country, returns home to his father saying, "Father, I have sinned against heaven and before you; I am no longer worthy to be called your son" (Lk. 15.21). This mention of heaven could be dismissed as a mere rhetorical flourish. But if being against heaven amounts to nothing unearthly but, on the contrary, amounts to being against the very way that life is now forthcoming toward us, then the word "sin" takes on a clear definition. To be set against the life currently forthcoming from God is to be set against not only oneself and one's own best interests, but against the life interests of all those with whom this forthcoming now brings one into relation. Being off course, in this sense, is sin against heaven.

Finally, in regard to heaven as the course of God's forthcoming, we even hear of waiting for new heavens and a new earth. In 2 Peter this reference to waiting is directed against those scoffers who make light of the promise of the Lord's coming, asking why the Lord is so slow. The new forthcoming is described as "where righteousness is at home" (2 Pet. 3.13). In other Gospel testimony, such as the vision given to John in the book of Revelation, reference is made to seeing "a new heaven and a new earth" when "the first heaven and the first earth had passed away, and the sea was no more" (Rev. 21.1). The vision to John is said to involve seeing that "the home (σκηνή, tent of dwelling) of God is among mortals (μετὰ τῶν ἀνθρώπων, with human beings)" (Rev. 21.3). Though somewhat differently expressed, the forthcoming of heaven is associated in these references, as in those already noted in 1 Kings, with the locus and focus of God's dwelling place. In the background is the prophecy of Isaiah that declares, "For as the new heavens and the new earth, which I will make, shall remain before me, says the Lord; so shall your descendants and your name remain" (Isa. 66.22). To our ears today such reported visions of a new heaven and a new earth may sound like some outdated science fiction. Or, it may sound like news that nothing facing us now or in the future, even in what the Psalmist calls "the terror of the night . . . or the destruction that wastes at noonday" (Ps. 91.5-6), will have the power to leave us abandoned as orphans before what is coming. "I will not leave you orphaned; I am coming to you" (Jn 14.18). Without attempting to harmonize the textual differences of these passages, we may detect in each, if we listen, the sound of "home," as God's new creation of dwelling with us that this new forthcoming of heaven and earth is said to bring with it. The new heaven or heavens, for which listeners to this testimony are directed to look and wait, is once again more than the sky, the hereafter, or a feeling of bliss. It sounds like nothing less than God taking a new course of action in coming events to make the kind of home with us that will ever prove to be the right home for us. In words from Black church tradition, "God makes a way out of no way."

2. Heaven as Created

A second set of soundings that we hear in the Gospel tells of the heaven God makes way for as God's creation. This kind of reference is familiar from the opening line of Genesis: "In the beginning God created the heavens and the earth" (Gen. 1.1).[20] It occurs prominently as well in the prophecy of Isaiah and in the Psalms. In Isaiah God is addressed in prayer with the words, "you have made heaven and earth" (Isa. 37.16) and characterized as the Lord "that created the heavens" (Isa. 42.5, 45.18) and that, as just noted above, will create "new heavens and a new earth" (Isa. 65.17, 66.22). From the Psalms we hear, "By the word of the Lord the heavens were made, and all their host by the breath of his mouth" (Ps. 32.6).

New Testament references identify the Psalmist's "word of the Lord" by which the heavens were made with the Word said to become flesh in Jesus Christ. As the opening verses of the Fourth Gospel put it, "In the beginning was the Word, and the Word was with God, and the Word was God . . . All things came into being through him . . . And the Word became flesh and lived among us" (Jn 1.1, 3, 14). Accordingly, what we also hear of Christ in the Colossians letter is that "in him all things in heaven and on earth were created . . . all things have been created through him and for him" (Col. 1.16). Similarly, yet again in a distinctive way, the writer of Hebrews refers to God's Son "through whom he also created the worlds" (Heb. 1.2). The words of Psalm 102.25 are then applied to the Lord Jesus Christ, "the Son:" "'In the beginning, Lord, you founded the earth, and the heavens are the work of your hands'" (Heb. 1.10). Thus, not only from the Old Testament, but also from the New, we hear of heaven as created. The historian Rufinus of Aquileia (345–410), one of our earliest sources for what later develops into the Apostles' Creed, writes that the creedal affirmation of faith in God the Father as "maker of heaven and earth" was implicit before it was actually made explicit in hearing the Gospel testimony that all things were made through God's Word in Jesus Christ, the Son.[21]

The comprehensive expression in the Bible for the whole of creation is "heaven and earth." In certain instances "the sea" also is mentioned (Acts 4.24, 14.15; Rev. 10.6, 14.7, 21.1). The opening account in Genesis tells of creation, not as God's own being, but as all that God, and only God, calls forth into being, saying, "Let there be" (Gen. 1.3 ff.). What we label the physical cosmos of earth, sea, and sky is clearly intended, as are its habitation and inhabitants, with humankind said to be made in God's image. But we also hear this cosmic creation of heaven and earth described in the Gospel message as encompassing "things visible and invisible, whether thrones or dominions or rulers or powers," plainly indicating that more than the visible world is included (Col. 1.16).

Augustine, writing in his *Confessions*, offers his "provisional understanding" that we hear in the first chapter of Genesis of a twofold creation of heaven and earth. The first creation "in the beginning," mentioned in verse 1, must have been of an invisible heaven and earth, because it is described as formless and void and covered in darkness. Only afterwards in verse 5 is mention made of the creation of day and night — and hence, of light and time. Following this we are given a second account of the creation of heaven and earth in verses 6-10. This second reference is to a visible, temporal heaven depicted as the firmament or dome of the sky separating the waters above and below, and overarching the formed earth.[22] To the first creation of the invisible heaven Augustine applies the Old Testament term "the heaven of heaven" (Deut. 10.14, Neh. 9.6), or "the highest heaven" (Ps. 113.6, 148.3). But whether this "provisional understanding" of a twofold creation of heaven and earth is exactly what "Moses" had in mind in delivering these words, Augustine acknowledges, he cannot with certainty say.[23] ("To guess it, puzzles scholars —.") Rather, Augustine concludes his speculations with prayer, expressing confidence that the Lord's intentions will be made clear either by this or by some other understanding of what is to be revealed in hearing the words of these texts.[24]

Hearers of heaven today may share with Augustine the situation of praying for a faithful understanding while not sharing his fourth-century context of Neoplatonic speculation. Without claiming more knowledge of the subject than knowing how the Gospel testimonies sound, certain implications of hearing of heaven as created may draw our attention. One is that, in this particular frame of reference, to say that God's forthcoming dwells in heaven is to say that God's forthcoming, while not itself creation, takes its course in creation. If this is the message, heaven is not reached by any flight from, or taking leave of, the world that is God's creation. Equally, if the created world, the *cosmos*, includes heaven, it is not reducible merely to any currently apparent scheme of things, that *schema* as Paul writes, which is "passing away" (1 Cor. 7.31). It follows from what we are hearing that the God of the Gospel chooses to exercise dominion by employing creaturely means. This is indeed what traditions of church teaching, in some form or another, have long affirmed. What may come more as news is that creation, if heaven is created, includes much more than meets the eye.

Yet we may detect all this and still hear nothing that approaches the apparent life-and-death importance expressed by the Psalmist's exultation, "Our help is in the name of the Lord, who made heaven and earth" (Ps. 124.8). If the sound of heaven as created serves to identify where help in life and death is to be found, then we obviously are not getting the message if by this testimony we hear only unhelpful talk of theoretical abstractions.

Puzzling over this brings us to a further recognition. There is plainly a difference at least to be noted between hearing that the earth is overarched by the sky, whether of an outdated cosmology or of modern space science, and hearing that the earth is overarched by an unimpeded dominion of love and freedom. Yet the latter may be said to follow from listening to the biblical accounts of creation in relation to the rest of the Gospel. In short, earth is depicted as having no other existence than "under heaven" (Deut. 4.19; Acts 2.5). Hope is promised to "every creature under heaven" (Col. 1.23). Heaven is said to be the "throne" (Ps. 11.4; Isa. 66.1; Mt. 5.34) where the will and way of the One characterized as "love" (1 Jn 4.8) and "freedom" (2 Cor. 3.17) is "established" (Ps. 103.19). Opposition to this dominion of love and freedom, which leads to its crucifixion on earth in the Cross of Jesus Christ, is graphically recounted in the vision given to John in Revelation as having already been defeated and thrown out of heaven. Originally addressed to those undergoing persecution or tempted by indifference in the late first century, this assurance is given that God's dominion is unimpeded in heaven:

> 7 And war broke out in heaven; Michael and his angels fought against the dragon. The dragon and his angels fought back, 8 but they were defeated, and *there was no longer any place for them in heaven*. 9 The great dragon was thrown down, that ancient Serpent, who is called the Devil and Satan, the deceiver of the whole world — he was thrown down to the earth, and his angels were thrown down with him (Rev. 12.7-9).

For its part, the Letter to the Ephesians admittedly does refer to its hearers' continuing struggle "against the spiritual forces of evil in the heavenly places" (Eph. 6.12). Nevertheless, it is equally emphatic that the power of Christ's resurrection in which they have been raised to the heavenly places is above every impediment, enabling them in the strength of this power now to "stand against the wiles of the devil," and "quench all the flaming arrows of the evil one" (Eph. 6.10-16). We may conclude that at least for those, then and now, for whom such a message rings true, the words of the Psalmist would hold more than an abstract or speculative resonance. The news, whether we may view it as credible or not, becomes that our help is in the name of the One who does not make *any* situation we face on earth, however threatening or devastating, to be without the overarching forthcoming of an unimpeded dominion of love and freedom.

3. *Heaven as a Community*

In a third set of Gospel references we encounter yet another sound of heaven as a community or society in which God does not reside alone but with heavenly creatures. Today we may hear this ancient talk, with its traceable parallels in antiquity, as nothing more than an archaic and dispensable mythology. Or it may sound to us that it carries an import more accountable as a current state of affairs and arguably a scenario of life in the real world. In any case, at least we can say that a population of heaven seems to be indicated. This population of creatures accompanying God's exercise of dominion from heaven toward earth is commonly referred to scripturally as a "heavenly host." "The sun, the moon, and the stars" are said to comprise this host (Deut. 4.19), as are the "angels" and indeed all heavenly creatures that serve to carry out God's will (Ps. 103.21). Prophets are reported to hear the word of the Lord as envisioning "the Lord sitting on his throne, with all the host of heaven standing to the right and to the left of him" (2 Chron. 18.18). In the night vision of Daniel regarding the heavenly throne the testimony is, "A thousand thousands served him, and ten thousand times ten thousand stood attending him" (Dan. 7.10). To many Protestant churchgoers of the past this sound may most routinely have been conveyed through the weekly singing of the familiar doxology,

> Praise God from whom all blessings flow.
> Praise Him all creatures here below.
> Praise Him above, *ye heavenly host.*
> Praise Father, Son, and Holy Ghost.

A similar note occurs in the liturgical ascription of praise historically heard in most Christian churches, "Therefore *with angels and archangels, and with all the company of heaven,* we laud and magnify Thy glorious name."

However the heavenly population is characterized, a consistent theme attending its mention in the Bible and the worship of the church is that this company solely reflects God's glory and is not to be worshiped itself. There is no pantheism here of heaven or of earth. In 2 Kings especially, as in its parallels in 2 Chronicles, we hear of the "worship" of "all the host of heaven" condemned as idolatry (2 Kings 17.16, 21.3-5, 23.4-5; 2 Chron. 33.3-5). Rather, the Psalmist sings, "Let the heavens praise your wonders, O Lord, your faithfulness in the assembly of the holy ones," asking, "For who in the skies can be compared to the Lord? Who among the heavenly beings is like the Lord" (Ps. 89.5-6)? The clearest summary statement of this sounding may perhaps be heard in the prayer of Ezra recounted in Nehemiah: "You are the Lord, you alone; you have made heaven, the heaven of heavens, with all their host, the earth and all that is on it, the seas and all that is in them. To all of them you give life, and the host of heaven worships you" (Neh. 9.6).

This communal character of heaven is denoted by Paul in his Letter to the Philippians with the use of the Greek word *politeuma* (πολίτευμα). Paul writes, "But our *politeuma* is in heaven, and it is from there that we are expecting a Savior, the Lord Jesus Christ" (Phil. 3.20). The word *politeuma*, as well as the cognate Greek noun *politeia*, may be translated into English as either "commonwealth" or "citizenship," and one finds both translations used. Both have to do with government, hence our derived English word *politics*. Each contributes a distinctive nuance within the context of hearing the Gospel.

For example, the announcement that "our *commonwealth* is in heaven" sounds as if God's dwelling, or, so to speak, God's whereabouts, is not in isolation but with a blessed company of creaturely wellbeing whom God chooses not to be without. This is similar to the communal note of the Old Testament texts that tell of a heavenly host. In this instance, moreover, what is added is that those addressed by Paul's announcement are told that they themselves, at least in some respect, presently belong to this heavenly commonwealth. Furthermore, the announcement that "our *citizenship* is in heaven" extends the metaphorical import of this reference to include news of where the current rights and responsibilities of the hearers in their earthly situations now come from. The hearers' right to exist on earth, the legitimacy of their being who they are and where they are as God's creation upon the earth, is said not to derive from any earthly authority but from an authority coming from heaven. A somewhat similar note also occurs in Paul's Letter to the Galatians, where those faithful to the Gospel are told that their true freedom currently derives, not from any authority exercised, or status conferred, by the present, earthly Jerusalem, but from "the Jerusalem above." This community of a heavenly Jerusalem that, like Sarah, is said to engender and legitimate a faithful following of God's promise now on earth is in this second instance referred to by Paul as "our mother" (Gal. 4.26).[25] One may only conclude that any listeners, then or now, struggling for survival, whose legitimate right to exist is being denied or seriously questioned by the principalities and powers of the present age, might reasonably receive this announcement as good news.

That heaven makes a political difference, as suggested by the words *politeuma* and *politeia*, would seem to sound undeniable, though exactly what the political consequences are has been a subject of dispute in Christian history. The Letter to the Ephesians, for example, admittedly calls upon slaves to obey their earthly masters and yet at the same time reminds earthly masters in relating to their slaves that "both of you have the same Master in heaven" with whom "there is no partiality" (Eph. 6.5, 9). Staying simply with the Gospel soundings at this point, attention to the Philippians text does show Paul making a connection between heaven as a commonwealth granting the right of citizenship and how such citizens of heaven are now free to conduct their lives on earth. Those listening to the epistle read aloud, as was the custom, would have heard a verbal form of the same Greek word that we miss in English translation: "Only live your life (πολιτεύεσθε, *politeuesthe*, govern yourselves) in a manner worthy of the gospel of Christ" (Phil. 1.27). The call to follow the good news of Christ in this scriptural context may in effect be heard to translate into, "Govern your life according to the governing of heaven." If the "Master in heaven" governs every mastery and obedience on earth, it sounds as if all established relationships of earthly dominance and domination are radically subverted.

The "citizenship" metaphor of Philippians is picked up later by the unknown author of the so-called Epistle to Diognetus, a laudatory defense of early Christians, arguably dating from about the third century. The account given of the Christians reads,

> Yet while living in Greek and barbarian cities, according as each obtained his lot, and following the local customs, both in clothing and food and in the rest of life, they show forth the wonderful and confessedly strange character of the constitution of their own citizenship (*politeias*) . . . Their lot is cast "in the flesh" but they do not live "after the flesh." They pass their time upon the earth, but they have their citizenship in heaven (*en ourano politeuontai*).[26]

Running through all these varied references to heaven as a community is a recurring note of heaven's proximity to what is currently happening on earth. This should not go undetected. Contrary to more conventional projections of a "sweet by and by" reserved for later, it sounds as if a company of heaven is somehow involved, even indispensably involved, in what is actually taking place here and now.

In this connection we hear of the heavenly "angels." "Do not neglect to show hospitality to strangers," is a word of advice from the Letter to the Hebrews, "for thereby some have entertained angels unawares" (Heb. 13.2). The reminder that the hearers of the Hebrews letter may unexpectedly be having dealings with angels and not recognizing it suggests that, however artfully we may imagine them, angels, at least in the context of scriptural usage, may be said not to call attention to themselves. Being representatives of heaven, they do not represent themselves but attest to the Lord of heaven whose forthcoming they accompany. Karl Barth's term for them as God's "entourage" of heavenly "ambassadors" is apt.[27] Our unawareness of them, it would seem, counters any attempts to classify the Gospel's references to angels simply as our poetic constructs or the figments of our imagination. The etymological association of their name *angelos* (ἄγγελος) with news, *angelia* (ἀγγελία), further suggests the biblical role ascribed to them as messengers and announcers. In today's more popular jargon, we may even hear of heavenly angels without trivialization as news media in the sense that they are depicted as the unimpeded creaturely means serving to transmit the news event of God's forthcoming. The relation of their creaturely mediacy to heaven and earth, we are told, is one of "ascending and descending" frequency in the service of God's purposes (Gen. 28.12, Jn 1.51).

Evil angels are also mentioned in Gospel testimony. They are characterized as enemies of God's purposes that have thereby forfeited their mediacy to heaven. For these defeated angels of the devil in their battle in heaven against Michael and his angels, the vision given to John in the book of Revelation, as we have noted, foretells "no longer any place for them in heaven" (Rev. 12.8). They have been thrown down, with their destructiveness now confined to earth in company, not with heaven, but with the evil adversary described in 1 Peter as "like a roaring lion . . . [that] prowls around, looking for someone to devour" (1 Pet. 5.8). From the Letter of Jude we hear of "the angels who did not keep their own position, but left their proper dwelling" for the "chains" of judgment (Jude 1.6). In 2 Peter the association of the sinful angels is said to be with "hell" (ταρταρώσας) (2 Pet. 2.4). What is extraordinary is that within the soundings of this scriptural context of usage, we hear of no symmetry between the angels in company with heaven and the angels in company with hell. Heaven and hell are not spoken of as equal opposites on a par. In contrast to what is said to be coming to pass from heaven, the devil's time is described as "short" (Rev. 12.12). As such, it sounds more like part of "the form of this world" said by Paul to be "passing away" (1 Cor. 7.31). Unlike earth, we do not hear of hell as a counterpart of heaven.[28] While earth is overarched by heaven, hell is depicted as overtaken.

4. *Heaven as a* Basileia *at Hand*

We return now to the most prominent references to heaven heard in the Gospel message, those that associate heaven with a coming *basileia* announced as being "at hand." This fourth set of references resounds as the most comprehensive, in that the three others we have noted — heaven as the course of God's forthcoming, as created, and as a community — all find expression here.

Once again, the sound of heaven's proximity as an arriving state of affairs is emphatic. According to Mark's Gospel, Jesus' announcement that God's heavenly *basileia* is at hand begins with saying that "the time is fulfilled" (Mk 1.15). To the scribe who confesses the love of God and neighbor to be much more important than burnt offerings and sacrifices, Jesus is reported to say, "You are not far from the *basileia* of God" (Mk 12.34). In Luke's account of the appointing of the seventy to go on ahead in pairs to every town and place where he himself is about to come, Jesus charges them to announce everywhere, "The *basileia* of God has come near to you" (Lk. 10.9, 11). To the Pharisees who question when God's *basileia* is coming, the answer from Jesus is given, "Notice (ἰδού), the *basileia* of God is in your midst (ἐντος ὑμων, among you)" (Lk. 17.20-21). Inasmuch as God's *basileia* at hand is proclaimed in the context of the Gospel testimony to be a *basileia* coming from heaven, the current proximity of heaven to earth must be acknowledged to be an unmistakable feature.

Yet on this point, how the New Testament scriptures tell of the kingdom's "at-handed-ness" is curiously different from our conventional ways of thinking about proximity. This is what makes the hearing of it today so fascinating. The message sounds equally clear and unmistakable that what is near at hand on earth as God's *basileia* from heaven taking place does not approximate, or conform to, any state of affairs that may be said to be already in hand, or in place. A whole history of philosophical empiricism is thereby called into question. Apparently included is any capacity we have as flesh and blood creatures to approximate this *basileia* conceptually by means of some prior frame of reference. *The proximity is without approximation.* Consistent with this is the honest philosopher Isaiah Berlin's reported statement shortly before his death in 1997 that heaven "made no sense in any conceptual scheme he knew."[29] No antecedent form of this world can accommodate the heavenly *basileia's* coming.

We hear this news announced in various ways. The *basileia's* coming is said not to be subject to public observation; "not coming with signs to be observed" is the Gospel of Luke's way of putting it. When it is among us, it does not lend itself, so we are told, to anyone's saying, "It's here," or, "It's there" (Lk. 17.20-21). "Flesh and blood cannot inherit" this *basileia*, so Paul writes to the Corinthians, any more than can that which is perishable and passing away be said to inherit, or be endowed with, what is imperishable and coming to pass (1 Cor. 15.50). In short, to cite the Fourth Gospel's rendering of the words of Jesus, "My *basileia* is not of [or from] this world (ἐκ του κόσμου)" (Jn 18.36).

To hear that heaven as a *basileia* comes to us in this world, but not as part of this world, would seem to leave us confounded by contradiction.

> And through a Riddle, at the last —
> Sagacity, must go —

Some have so concluded and therefore argued that what listeners to the Gospel should really be hearing in these testimonies is reference only to an inner world, a coming within one's heart and soul. "From this point of view everything dramatic in the external and historical sense has vanished; and gone too are all the external hopes for the future," wrote the influential interpreter of modern Christianity, Adolf Harnack, approvingly in 1900: "The kingdom of God comes by coming to the individual, by entering into his soul and laying hold of it . . . It is not a question of angels and devils, thrones and principalities, but of God and the soul, the soul and its God."[30] This internal reference was taken to be the kernel of the Gospel message by Harnack and others of similar persuasion because, once again, it was judged in 1900 to be more acceptable to the modern mind. Everything that was heard to be external was rejected as dispensable husk.

The problem with this proposal, however, is that the text of John 18.33-36, in which the saying of Jesus that his *basileia* is "not of [or from] this world" occurs, does not allow those who listen to it to avoid hearing precisely of "thrones and principalities" and, what Harnack dismissed as things "dramatic in the external and historical sense." In fact, it would be hard to find a clearer Gospel reference to the relation of heaven's *politeuma* to earthly politics.

Consider the textual context. Jesus, as depicted in this account, is on trial before Pontius Pilate and is interrogated about the charge of his accusers that he claims to be the king of the Jews. It is to this specific questioning under the governing authority of a historical ruler that the reply is made, "My *basileia* is not of this world." This reply is then followed in the Johannine text by the explanation that if Jesus' *basileia* were from this world, his followers would be fighting to keep him from being handed over, but that this world is not from whence his *basileia* derives (Jn 18.33-36). It is, however, the world to which his *basileia* comes. The One said in John's Gospel to be from heaven takes his place before Pontius Pilate, not simply as an internal drama of the soul apart from the time, space, and affairs of this earth with its "angels and devils, thrones and principalities." This *basileia* is indeed otherworldly in the sense that it refuses to engage the enemies of heaven's coming to earth on the enemies' own terms, or according to the enemies' schemes. But it does engage them on the same earthly scene *sub Pontio Pilato* where the actual ruling powers of opposition currently holding sway in this world's history conduct their trials. In this instance, the import certainly would seem to be that heaven does not come on its enemies' terms, but it does come on its enemies' turf in all of that turf's worldly dimensions, external as well as internal.

Within this frame of reference, death on earth in all of its annihilating powers, and not only as an inner death of the soul, is said to be subject to what comes from heaven. "The last enemy to be destroyed," Paul writes, "is death" (1 Cor. 15.26). In hearing that heaven is not restricted to an upperworld or afterlife, but is now at hand in the daily events of this earth, the news of the Gospel is equally clear that heaven's coming brings life beyond death. Heaven, as noted earlier, neither begins nor ends with death. The coming of life from heaven that we hear of in the Gospel testimonies holds priority over every power of death. As such it no more sounds confined to an interior state of mind than it sounds deferred to a postmortem hereafter. What is coming to pass from heaven is announced as now overtaking what is passing away on earth. This is the real world that hearers of this Gospel are told they now live in.

News of such a heavenly state of affairs at hand but not in hand is conveyed in the teaching of Jesus through parables, by pointing listeners to a significance in familiar situations of their day, not publicly observable as signs of heaven according to the listeners' prevailing perceptions. Matthew's Gospel states, "This is why I speak to them in parables, because seeing they do not see, and hearing they do not hear, nor do they understand" (Mt. 13.13). The coming of heaven is said to be *like* such ordinary, this-earthly realities as a sower of seed, a grain of mustard seed when it is sowed, leaven in bread, treasure hidden in a field, a merchant seeking pearls, a fishing net, a king seeking to settle accounts, a householder hiring laborers, a royal host inviting guests to a wedding feast, or ten bridesmaids with their lamps going at night to meet the bridegroom.[31] But, in this respect as well, we hear in the Gospel parables of a heavenly proximity to things of earth, and to current situations, that sounds as if it does not conform to any approximation of what listeners to this Gospel currently tend to take the real world to be. Parables are said to signify what is not immediately apparent (Lk. 19.11). Whatever riddle such a hearing poses to sagacity, if heaven in some sense is a state of affairs that takes place in our midst "like this," as the parables say, at once proximate or close to what is familiar, but not approximated in conformity to our preconceptions, this parabolic significance can only come to hearers then and now as astonishing news. We will return to reflect further on this subject of parabolic significance in Chapter 3.

From such soundings as these we are led to conclude that the word heaven primarily refers to nothing less than what are proclaimed to be the current conditions under which our life is really being lived. We may or may not find this way of speaking about "the real world" now taking place credible, but to hear of heaven in this scriptural context of discourse is certainly to hear news of what is announced at least to be the most inescapable reality now facing us, whatever the heights or depths of our present situation.

This first chapter on the hearing of heaven today is meant to be taken as a brief that summarizes testimony for further questioning and examination. The four sorts of Gospel references to heaven reported on here introduce us to a subject allegedly not reducible to the more conventional associations of heaven with the sky, a postmortem afterlife, or any induced ecstasy of blissful feelings. But news reports invite questioning, even ones accompanied by "Much Gesture from the Pulpit," and the Gospel traditions themselves call for it. The author of 1 John writes, "Beloved, do not believe every spirit, but test the spirits to see whether they are from God" (1 Jn 4.1). Paul's appeal to the Thessalonians is to "test everything" (1 Thess. 5.21).

> Narcotics cannot still the Tooth
> That nibbles at the soul —

To test this first chapter's reporting of the Gospel news regarding heaven requires that we turn now from the first to the second sense of hearing, auditing, or sounding — from listening only to also weighing what is heard.

Chapter 2

THE THEOLOGY OF HEAVEN

A hymn of the church that contains the words, "Faith believes, nor questions how,"[1] bears false witness to the Gospel as news. News always raises questions and is subject to questioning. Is what is reported trustworthy or not? Is it true? And if so, what kind of truthfulness makes it so? Theology as a discipline of study gives attention to such questions of credibility. In keeping with a biblical context of discerning true and false prophecy it examines what is being professed to be the case — which is the original meaning of the word "dogma" — by seeking to distinguish in such profession a trustworthy credibility from an untrustworthy credulity, a task of appraisal that thus comes to be referred to in theology as "dogmatics."

"What then are we to say to these things?," Paul asks the hearers of the Gospel in Rome (Rom. 8.31). We must now ask the same of the hearing of heaven just reported and consider how the Gospel talk of a heavenly *coming* said to be *at hand* may be trusted to make sense today.

It is instructive to note that a similar inquiry in theology at the turn of the last century gave rise to a trajectory of responses that now comprise one of the twentieth century's most important theological legacies. In this chapter we will look at four of these responses. They include the claims made about (1) hearing of heaven literally, (2) hearing of heaven as myth, (3) hearing of heaven as saga, and (4) hearing of heaven as promise. While students of theology will be familiar with the names of the theologians associated with these responses and the labels by which their thought is often characterized, the aim will be to reopen these four cases — by focusing attention upon the issues they pose without prejudging them according to conventional labeling or textbook classifications.

The inquiry in question emerged with the unsettling observations that came to coalesce from three figures, Johannes Weiss (1863–1914), Albert Schweitzer (1875–1965), and Franz Overbeck (1837–1905), each of whom wrote independently about the New Testament preaching of Jesus concerning a heavenly *basileia at hand* and how it had come to be disregarded by later generations. Their verdict was that there is a mistake of false expectations about heaven at the very heart of the Gospel.[2] The trajectory of the four contrasting responses we will consider attempts to address this startling verdict. The record in brief is as follows.

Convicting the News of Heaven

A controversy that greatly stirred Protestant theological circles a hundred years ago arose precisely over what to make of the Gospel testimony that God's *basileia* from heaven was at hand. It was commonly agreed that the message of the kingdom of God was central to the teaching attributed to Jesus in the New Testament. But the idea of a kingdom, or dominion, of God presently coming from heaven to displace what was taken to be "the real world" had increasingly come to be viewed by critical biblical scholars as an untrustworthy feature of the earliest Gospel preaching. The world, it seemed obvious, did not come to an end as expected, and ever since the testimony to a *basileia* of God now taking place from heaven, it was assumed, had to be altered. The husk of any external worldview in this testimony had to be dispensed with in order to retrieve whatever relevant kernel of internal spiritual truth this husk might contain for the modern age. Attempts were made to interpret such inner spiritual truth of the *basileia* of heaven as a matter of God coming only to the soul, and ruling within the believing heart and will. The kingdom of God could now be made intelligible only as our "purely inward" autonomous moral duty, the influential philosopher Immanuel Kant had persuasively argued, that was in process of realizing itself as an "ethical commonwealth" in society.[3] This represented a turn from cosmological categories of interpretation to anthropological ones in thinking about what any longer was trustworthy in the Gospel testimony to the *at-handedness* of heaven.

When the Gospel message of heaven's coming is taken to refer only to internal matters, in contrast to a wider world inclusive of more than the self, it is but a small step to classify its message under a generic label as "religious," a classification that is limiting, and even arguably foreign, to the Gospel message itself.[4] "Religion is," in Alfred North Whitehead's often-quoted words, "what the individual does with his own solitariness."[5] Or, as William James put it in 1902, "Religion" refers to "individual(s) . . . in their solitude . . . in relation to whatever they may consider the divine."[6] Weiss, Schweitzer, and Overbeck, in their differing ways, each argued that this accommodation to an inner so-called spiritual or moral world of "God and the soul" could not claim to represent "the real world" in its fullness as envisaged in the original Gospel teaching. "The Kingdom of God as Jesus thought of it is never something subjective, inward, or spiritual," Johannes Weiss wrote in 1892, "but is always the objective messianic Kingdom, which usually is pictured as a territory into which one enters, or as a land in which one has a share, or as a treasure which comes down from heaven."[7]

Weiss was equally forthright that the *basileia* from heaven in the teaching of Jesus did not refer to any kingdom built by human moral effort. In stark contrast to modern interpretations like those of Kant, and later of Albrecht Ritschl, his own father-in-law, Weiss boldly states that "the notion of an 'actualization of the Rule of God' by human ethical activity is completely contrary to the transcendentalism of Jesus's idea."[8] This *basileia* cannot be equated with any currently established cultural constructions, either of the church or of society. "The real difference between our modern Protestant world-view and that of primitive Christianity," Weiss concluded, is "that we do not share the . . . attitude . . . [as Paul expressed it] that 'the form of this world is passing away'" (1 Cor. 7.31). The modern mind no longer takes the heavenly *basileia* to be, in Weiss's words, "a counter," in the sense of a countervailing force, "to this present age [*den* αἰὼν οὗτος *verneinend*]."[9] This was the compelling point. Nevertheless, in the opinion of Weiss, and of Schweitzer as well, such an accommodation in worldview still qualified as Christianity, though it could not rightly be said to be the Gospel teaching of Jesus. The result was that, contrary to Jesus' teaching, the coming of the kingdom could no longer be credibly heard of as something that takes place from heaven, but now only remained trustworthy instead as a matter of ethics, "something which has to be realized."[10] Weiss's conclusion in 1892 regarding the Gospel's *basileia* teaching was that today we can only "use it in a different sense from Jesus," and seek "the kernel of our systematic theology . . . not [in] his idea of the Kingdom of God, but that of the religious and ethical fellowship of the children of God."[11] "What he had expected," Schweitzer wrote of Jesus, "did not occur."[12]

It was an extraordinary about-face. Having first judged the prevailing modern interpretation of the heavenly *basileia* as prominently espoused by Kant and some of the foremost theology of the time influenced by him to be antithetical to the Gospel message itself, Weiss then concedes that the modern-day Christian, notwithstanding, has no creditable alternative but to accept it. Rudolf Bultmann was later to study with Weiss.[13]

For the even more radical Overbeck, in contrast, such accommodation, inevitable though it may have been, rendered the primal witness of the Gospel testimony, and what was most distinctive about it, null and void. What was preached, wrote Overbeck, was the end of the world, and what resulted when this did not occur was the end of what was authentically Christian and the beginning of something totally alien to this preaching, an ongoing historical development that we label "Christianity."[14] "Neither Christ himself," to quote Overbeck, "nor the faith which he found(ed) among his disciples has ever had any historical existence at all under the name of Christianity."[15] For Overbeck it is the emergence of historical Christianity itself that represents the break with Gospel faith and, in this sense, everything that has followed since the second century has been a pseudo-Christian age. Karl Barth was later to acknowledge his indebtedness to the provocation of Overbeck.[16]

My purpose in recalling the names of Johannes Weiss, Albert Schweitzer, and Franz Overbeck is simply to remind us that there were those at the beginning of the last century who recognized that what the so-called modern mind took to be "the real world" was radically different from what is taken to be "the real world" in the Gospel testimony of God's *basileia* of heaven at hand. Their position in emphasizing this difference in perspective, however, was not to deny the modern way of interpreting the world. Indeed, they took the modern world's frame of reference as the only creditable one for their time. A countervailing state of affairs arriving on the scene from heaven may have been what the original hearers of Jesus got from his message. But nearly two thousand years later such a view of heaven as supposedly a counterforce to whatever captivating powers currently are holding sway over the present age, they each concluded, cannot be said to represent "the real world" in the modern scheme of things. Unlike Paul's day, we think of "passing away" not in regard to the "form of this world," but individually.

It is plain that the question addressed by this critical, and in some ways still commendable, reflection of the last century was: *What is no longer believable or trustworthy in the Gospel talk of heaven, given the modern frame of reference?* Today, the reverse question calls for equal consideration: *What is no longer believable or trustworthy in the modern frame of reference, given the Gospel talk of heaven?*

Our curiosity, if not suspicion, may be aroused when we come to the end of Weiss's text, *Jesus' Proclamation of the Kingdom of God,* and notice how he characterizes what he calls "our modern Protestant world-view."[17] Having first emphasized that, "The Kingdom of God as Jesus thought of it is never something subjective, inward, or spiritual, but is always the objective messianic Kingdom, which usually is pictured as a territory into which one enters, or as a land in which one has a share, or as a treasure which comes down from heaven," Weiss then writes in contrast:[18]

> We no longer pray, "May grace come and the world pass away," but we pass our lives in the joyful confidence that *this* world will evermore become the showplace of the people of God . . . The world will further endure, but we, as individuals, will soon leave it . . . We do not await a Kingdom of God which is to come down from heaven to earth and abolish this world, but we do hope to be gathered with the church of Jesus Christ into the heavenly βασιλεία [*basileia*].

This about-face prompts us to reopen the question of what is meant in this statement by the term "world." Is it the planet, the cultural era of the late nineteenth and prewar twentieth century in which Weiss was writing, or the "principalities and powers" of which we hear in Ephesians 6.12 that are said to be seeking to dominate current affairs? In what sense is it that the "modern Protestant world-view" claims that *this* world is not passing away before the coming of heaven, and that the Gospel is mistaken in proclaiming such? At the end we are left once again with the idea of heaven, not as a state of affairs coming to pass, but as our individual passing away from earth, and leaving it for an afterlife, or hereafter, as the church gathered into a heavenly *basileia*. But is this the news to be heard today in the Gospel?

The case argued by Weiss, and other definers of a faithful modernity in the last century, that a central message of the Gospel is mistaken, in that "we do not await a Kingdom of God which is to come down from heaven to earth and abolish this world," today provides grounds of appeal for a retrial of testimony leading to the verdict and conviction as to who is, and who is not, as the saying goes, "living in the real world." But today, with a twenty-first century upsurge in end of the world and apocalyptic scenarios once again grasping the public imagination and exerting surprising geopolitical influence, appealing the decision alleging the Gospel's big mistake of false expectations in its news of heaven cannot simply be a matter of dismissing the legacy of Weiss, Schweitzer, and Overbeck. Rather, we must reopen the question of the big mistake, and ask where it lies.

Retrying the News of Heaven

The thought experiment proposed in Chapter 1 is an attempt to undertake this retrial without claiming for itself any authoritative proof. Indeed, if heaven is the kind of forthcoming we have reported, it alone can serve to author its own vindication and prove itself to be so. In this case, however, non-authoritative need not mean inconsequential. What we can do is bear witness to what follows from hearing the Gospel news in this way and give an account of the difference that it makes. With the testimony as presented in Chapter 1 serving as our brief, this difference in real-life terms may be said to sound, at least, like it is of the utmost consequence.

Since 1892, when Weiss first published his findings, more than a century of books and articles have continued to be written about the Gospel references to God's heavenly *basileia*. An extensive scholarly literature of conflicting testimony and theological debate addresses the significance of such references, usually with at least footnote citations to Weiss, Schweitzer, and Overbeck, under the rubrics of the eschatological and apocalyptic aspects of scriptural testimony. In this trajectory of reflection one finds such classifications used to differentiate eschatological positions as "realized," "futurist," and "transcendental," in disputes over whether God's proclaimed heavenly *basileia* announced as now at hand is more coherently to be understood as evolving out of the past or as intervening from the future, as primarily immanent or as imminent, as internal to the soul or external, and as continuous with historical developments as we know them or discontinuous. There are critics as well who question whether such so-called eschatological or apocalyptic significance should even be attributed to Jesus's own teaching, as Weiss, Schweitzer, and Overbeck contended, or rather has been imposed upon his more sage-like wisdom sayings by later New Testament redactors.

Outside this arena of specialized academic theology, and exercising a far greater influence upon sectors of the general public in recent decades, are the more popularized, often fundamentalist, portrayals of the end times available from books, films, and Internet sites that graphically do depict a coming from heaven at hand that abolishes this world "left behind."[19] These dramatic, often sensational, portrayals represent a rejection of the so-called "modern Protestant world-view" and its attempts to internalize the Gospel references to heaven and instead cast the apocalyptic visions of the biblical books of Daniel, the Synoptic Gospels,[20] and Revelation as predictions to be fulfilled literally as facts of world history. Biblical prophecy is equated with predictions of coming events that are projected to occur through a series of historical periods or "dispensations" revealing a world of sin destined for destruction leading to Christ's imminent return just prior to the millennium envisioned in Revelation 20 of a thousand-year reign on earth.

The intellectual roots of these self-described "fundamentalist," "premillennialist," and "dispensationalist" interpretations of heaven's coming may be seen in the nineteenth-century teaching of John Nelson Darby in Britain, with its schematizations of God's "dispensations" in history, that came to prominence in certain circles of American evangelical revivalism and its opposition to modern critical theology in the early 1900s.[21] A widely popular later example in this tradition is the premillennialist account by Hal Lindsey, described by one critic as "the author of what may be the best-selling book of the late twentieth century, *The Late Great Planet Earth.*"[22]

Trials and retrials require knowledge of the records. But they also seek a verdict. With so much testimony on record in the background regarding the Gospel news of heaven, and so broad a range of subjects related to eschatological and apocalyptic themes, we turn now specifically to the four ways that figure most prominently in twentieth-century proposals for responding to the question of how this news can be considered trustworthy today.

1. *Hearing of Heaven Literally*

One initial response has been to say that the Gospel's news of heaven is, or is not, to be taken literally. The sense this makes in either case obviously depends upon what is meant by "literally," but the meaning of "literal" in the history of theology proves not to be as obvious as our ready use of the word may suggest. It derives from the phrase "according to the letter," and the letter of a text was typically said to denote its plain or seemingly common sense, as verbatim explicit statement, in contrast to any implicit meaning or allegorical sense that the "spirit" of a text might also convey. This distinction between a so-called literal and a spiritual reading dates back in antiquity to the interpreters of the Homeric tales of the gods and was articulated in Christian theology by Origen of Alexandria in the third century.[23] A medieval axiom of biblical interpretation contrasted literal references with what might be made of a text allegorically or morally "according to the spirit" of the scriptural passage by saying that the letter tells of deeds or happenings, *Littera gesta docet.*[24] It reports the facts.

According to today's most common way of reckoning, biblical literalism assumes that all reported world happenings to be actual must be factual historical happenings. Traditionally, the "literal sense" has also been called the "historical sense," though history has not always carried its modern requirements for documentation. Reports of what happens are taken to be referring to facts in the same, or univocal, sense of the word, regardless of their specific contexts. Reference is treated as contextually invariant. Really to climb Jacob's ladder literally means to go up a stepladder (Gen. 28.12). For news of heaven's coming to be true, it is argued, its taking place must be a historical fact as distinct from fiction. Truth is equated with what is factual and not fictional. Describing biblical prophecies as "predictions of exact historical happenings," Hal Lindsey, for example, writes that they are fulfilled "literally" in that they retain "the normal meaning understood by the people of the time in which [they were] written."[25] Literal in this univocal sense of "exact historical happenings" is thus assumed to be the norm for how the original hearers of the Gospel's news of heaven's coming understood it as well as the norm for how this news is properly to be heard today. A series typical of premillenialist publications interpreting heaven's coming as forecast in world events earlier appeared in England in 1840–1841 under the title of *The Literalist*.[26] The Gospel talk of heaven, by this accounting, is like the reporting or predicting of any other fact. To hear that a *basileia* is coming from heaven to earth to displace, or abolish, the form of this world that is passing away is logically the same as hearing that a meteor is coming from the sky to abolish the planet. For this reason, what is usually meant today by "literal" is more exactly to be described and assessed as *univocal* significance. This is how it is most popularly understood today.

Beyond this univocal type of literalism, which we usually think of when the term is applied today, it should also be acknowledged that theological interpretation from earliest times has also recognized that "according to the letter" some testimony itself employs parables, promises, or figurative ways of speaking that do not correspond simply to uniformly understood, or univocally defined, states of affairs or happenings.[27] To say that you will always be in my heart does not mean that open-heart surgery would find you there. To climb Jacob's ladder in the explicit dream context of the angels in Genesis 28.12 is not to go up a stepladder. These ways of speaking, while still "according to the letter," are not meant to be taken as referring to establishable facts. Thus, the literal sense in this more nuanced way of reckoning is said to stand for whatever the author of the testimony intended, whether it be a univocal factual reference or a figurative way of speaking. Authorial intent is thus a second way of defining the term. If the author intends to be understood by way of metaphor, analogy, parable, or some allegorical simile rather than historical fact, that is its literal meaning. Thomas Aquinas, who rejected the idea that references to the course of God's forthcoming from heaven were meant to be understood univocally,[28] nevertheless held that a faithful accounting rested upon the literal sense of scripture as authorial intent. Yet, Thomas argued further that insofar as such scripture conveys to faith sacred teaching we confess that the ultimate author is God. The literal sense as God's authorial intent thus is open to significance beyond the limited awareness of any of its human authors.[29] Later interpreters will speak similarly of a text's *tendency* that is not reducible simply to its human author's original *intent*.[30] Thus the so-called "literal significance" or "plain sense" of the Gospel talk of heaven has been thought of not only in terms of contextually invariant univocal reference, but also of authorial intent, and, most especially, of what God as the ultimate author intends its sacred teaching for its hearers to be.

Still further to be noted, in the third place, is a definition of "literal" as the meaning that a text or discourse communicates within the context or frame of reference that is native to it. Just as any language may be said to communicate and make sense by abiding by the rules of its own grammar, so the *sensus literalis* of the Gospel talk of heaven is said to be the intratextual usage, or semiotic functioning, intrinsic to this particular way of speaking. The literal meaning in this third instance is not held to come from any extratextual reference of factual correspondence or authorial intent.[31] We shall look more at this third way of defining the literal sense when we come to the topic of saga.

Considerations such as these figure prominently, not only in theological interpretation, but in jurisprudence as well, as witnessed today in debates between so-called "strict constructionists," or self-styled "textualists" such as U. S. Supreme Court Justice Antonin Scalia, who allow for only original meanings, and those who interpret the constitution as a living document whose full import only becomes known with respect to changing circumstances.[32]

Most questionable for our inquiry here and at issue today is the first rendering of "literal" as "univocal." When Johannes Weiss writes that as moderns "we do not await a Kingdom of God which is to come down from heaven to earth and abolish this world," and fundamentalists counter that they *do* await such a coming, both are assuming a contextually invariant univocal meaning. Merely disputing whether heaven's coming does or does not happen fails to address the more basic question of what such "happening" is heard to be in the Gospel's frame of reference as news.

Let us compare now this univocal literalism with the four sounds of heaven as set forth in Chapter 1. If we do hear of heaven as the course of God's forthcoming, and as a *basileia* or dominion that is proclaimed to be *at hand* but not in hand with any form or *schema* of this world that is passing away, this apocalyptic distinction between what is coming to pass in contrast to what is passing away, or between what is taking place in contrast to what is already in place, does not comply with what the theologian Ernst Troeltsch in 1898 called a "univocity of historical events."[33] That is, these are not states of affairs in the same way. The "course of this world" (Eph. 2.2) is not the directional course of God's heavenly forthcoming. According to the Gospel reports, whenever "the time is fulfilled" for earthly events it is the coming of heaven that fills it and not any emergence deriving from the earth itself. So too, if we hear of heaven as created, and as a community and *politeia* of a count-less host, it is not reported that this heavenly creation and citizenry are subject to the created time and space conditions of earth. Rather, it is the earth that is reported to be overarched by the arrival of the created time and space conditions opened up from heaven. Heaven's actual coming to pass is proclaimed as overtaking all that is factually passing away. From this Gospel frame of reference as news today, what sounds most real about the earth and the lifetime of all its inhabitants is actually heaven.

Most especially is this overarching by heaven heard to be the case with respect to the lack of parity in the Gospel message between heaven and hell. While scriptural references to heaven and earth tell of a creation in which earth is under heaven, even more so they tell of a redemption in which hell is rendered powerless before the keys of the coming *basileia* of heaven (Mt. 16.18-19). Contrary to any idea that heaven and hell are equally optional alternative states of affairs that can be actualized somehow by our decisions, it is precisely when beclouded by the direst forebodings and fear of the powers of heaven being shaken that hearers of the Gospel are told, in the reported words of Jesus, to lift up their heads because "redemption is drawing near" (Lk. 21.28).

In this hearing, what will be the case at the coming of Christ from heaven is not, as Hal Lindsey's literalism proposes, "exactly what hap-pens to those who are in a thermonuclear blast."[34] Quite the opposite of a univocal literalism, what is coming to pass and what is passing away are not heard of as the same order of happenings. Heaven, as what is coming to pass, overtakes in both its judgment and its hope all that is passing away. In the Lord's descent from heaven, as Paul writes of it to the Thessalonians in the words, "Then we who are alive, who are left, will be caught up in the clouds together with them [those who have died] to meet the Lord in the air; and so we will be with the Lord forever," there is no mention in this account of rapture of anyone being left behind (1 Thess. 4.15-17).

Taking the news of heaven literally, in the contextually invariant sense of univocally, thus shows itself in these respects not to be trustworthy or in keeping with the Gospel message.

2. Hearing of Heaven as Myth

The most commonly accepted twentieth-century alternative to a univocal literalism has been the position that the Gospel's news of heaven is to be recognized as myth. In this second proposal, as well as in the first, the case made with respect to such alleged mythic significance has not been as clear-cut as it at first may appear. While there is basic agreement here, as in most of modern theology, on the point of opposition to a univocal literalism, disagreement arises over how dispensable myth is in conveying this heavenly news. On this issue the influential positions of Rudolf Bultmann and Paul Tillich provide contrasting testimony, with Bultmann asserting the more negative role played by myth, and Tillich, the more positive.[35]

Among the ancient Greeks *mythos* denoted the primal stories of the gods from which philosophers sought to distill less anthropomorphic and more rationally creditable general principles. Aristotle, for example, uses the word "theology" in denoting both the stories of nectar and ambrosia that Hesiod and other poets tell in characterizing immortal beings (mythology) and also the higher theoretical science of causality necessary for reasoning about the ultimate nature of things (metaphysics).[36] With the rise of historical textual criticism in the seventeenth century the term "myth" becomes increasingly used for biblical stories judged not to be historically factual. All events not attributable to an earthly space and time nexus as univocally defined were thus classified as mythical. This obviously included all news of the acts of God or of any agency reported to derive from heaven. The Genesis accounts of God creating heaven and earth thus fall into this category of myth. So do the accounts of any of God's dealings from heaven, such as the inbreaking of a new kingdom. As far as Christian creedal affirmations are concerned, the only historically documented, and thus explicitly nonmythical, reference in this respect is to Pontius Pilate, whom Jesus is confessed to have "suffered under."

So-called "form criticism" of the scriptures further demonstrates the parallels between the accounts of the Old and New Testaments, and the mythic forms of expression of the ancient cultures in which these accounts originated. In the case of the original preaching [*kerygma*] of the Gospel's news, for example, the format, so Rudolf Bultmann wrote in 1941, reflects the worldview of Jewish apocalyptic and Gnostic redemption myths prevalent in the Middle Eastern environment of the first century.[37] Such a mythic format was judged to distort the true content of this news by serving to associate the hearing of heaven with an objectified cosmos, the top tier of a three-story worldview. Rather, Bultmann contends, the *kerygma* addresses its hearers not as cosmic spectators but as existing subjects with a call to abandon the false security such objectification provides and "find security only in the unseen beyond, in God."[38] This call to personal decision and new self-understanding is of a different order of engagement from simply subscribing to an objective worldview.

Hence, in Bultmann's key theme, "myth should be interpreted not cosmologically, but anthropologically, or better still, existentially."[39] Though the content of the news of heaven is not factual in a literalistic historical sense, it represents the kind of truth that is most historic for the individual in the personal or existential sense of "true to life." It is precisely this existential truth of the *kerygma* which addresses its hearers as living subjects that is masked today by the objectifying cosmological assumptions of the mythic worldviews of earliest Christianity in which this preaching was first formatted. To know the true content, to hear truly the Gospel news of the real heaven, one has therefore to differentiate it today from the form in which it originated; or, in Bultmann's signature term, one has to "demythologize" the Gospel message.

Three issues appear today to have been posed most pointedly by the advocacy of demythologization.

First is the understanding that to demythologize is to deliteralize from a univocal sense. On this initial point we find complete agreement between Bultmann and Tillich. To hear literally the Gospel news of heaven as expressed in the form of first-century cosmic myth is to mistake the truth of this news's content.

Second, to deliteralize is to require redescription of the Gospel news of heaven from a mythically objectified worldview into a non-objectifiable self-understanding of personal existence; that is, from a cosmological happening to an existential happening. The news which myth visualizes as an objective cosmological occurrence against a three-tiered backdrop of heaven above, hell below, and a flat earth in between reveals its true content only when it occurs existentially as a lived event involving its hearers as subjects of a new self-understanding and a new way of being. On this second point regarding redescription we find agreement as well, but now also the emergence of a difference over the scope of such existential happenings. Tillich's existentialism allows for more ontological claims, expressed as symbolic descriptions of the being of God and creation, in systematically interpreting a full range of Christian doctrines while Bultmann's rejects the necessity of such systematic symbolic interpretation and focuses more exclusively upon individual self-understanding, explicitly limiting any description of divine action to analogies of personal encounter.[40] For Bultmann, word that God is forthcoming from heaven is thus redescribed existentially to mean that I, the hearer of this news as presenting Jesus Christ, now understand myself to be personally addressed and called forth in response to trust above all else this Word-presence that "comes from heaven" (Jn 3.31).

Third is the question of the dispensability of mythic form to the Gospel content of heaven's coming, and here we find a clear disagreement. For Bultmann, though contending that his aim was "not to eliminate the mythological statements but to interpret them,"[41] the mythical articulation as such becomes dispensable, the discardable shell, following its deliteralized redescription in a true hearing of the *kerygma*: "As for mythology in its original sense, I maintain not only that we can dispense with it, but that it is essential to do so."[42] For Tillich deliteralized myth functions as the seedbed of religious symbolism and as such remains indispensable for providing the only language "able to express the ultimate."[43] It is the essential "vehicle" of symbolic expression necessary, in Tillich's words, to "the experience of the holy" whose removal "must be strongly rejected."[44]

Existential redescriptions of the Gospel significance of heaven, from objectifying cosmological happenings to non-objectifying anthropological or personal happenings, have subsequently come to be faulted for interpreting the news of heaven too exclusively in terms of the self in disregard of a wider social and political world.[45] Both Bultmann and Tillich denied that existential events were to be considered merely subjective, since it is precisely the news of heaven — *kerygma* for Bultmann, symbolization for Tillich — that is not subject to our creation or control as a product of our subjectivity. Yet in each case the sense of any cosmic and political eventfulness associated with heaven, whether as the course of God's forthcoming, or creation, or community as *politeia*, or an imminent *basileia*, tends to be either explicitly rejected or downplayed.

For Bultmann, cosmic and political conceptions mistake the *kerygmatic* news of God's actions.[46] For Tillich as well, to hear that "God is in heaven" does not mean that God "lives in" or "descends from" a special place, but rather that God's life is "qualitatively different from creaturely existence."[47] The mythical suggestion of a spatial locale becomes reformulated in a deliteralized hearing of the Gospel message to symbolize heaven as an experiential "state" and "basis" of blessedness.[48] Yet, in contrast to Bultmann's account, Tillich's retention of deliteralized myth as indispensable to symbolic expression of the ultimate enables him to give more of a hearing to aspects of biblical testimony that relate personal existence to a wider social world beyond the self. This becomes most evident in his discussion of the Kingdom of God in volume three of his *Systematic Theology*, where he writes that "again and again in later times people have found their own historical existence described in the mythical imagery of the apocalyptics," including "the inner-historical appearance of Jesus as the Christ."[49] This more positive retention of deliteralized apocalyptic myth in his third volume leads Tillich, while characterizing the *basileia* of heaven as an existential symbol, to allow for hearing, not of some transcendental and static state divorced from current affairs, but of a "dynamic power on earth for the coming of which we pray" that is "struggling with the demonic forces which are powerful in churches as well as empires."[50] A critical question is whether Tillich's preference for the redescription into existential symbolism of what he here calls "the mythical imagery of the apocalyptics" adequately takes account of the narrative and promissory aspects of the Gospel's apocalyptic testimony regarding heaven's coming.

What can be concluded is that for both Bultmann and Tillich, granting their differences, the recognition of the Gospel's news of heaven as myth represents a necessary transitional step in hearing its true content. While biblical references to heaven's forthcoming, creation, community, and *basileia* are often expressed cosmologically in terms of the time and space conditions of earth, they tell of a heaven that is said to be over the earth and forthcoming to life on earth. Thus the cosmological terms are not to be taken univocally as the literalists erroneously contend, but must be deliteralized and redescribed to fit the true to life conditions of our human existence, our way of being who we are.

But does such existential redescription impose its own alien framework upon the hearing of heaven as to what these true to life conditions are?[51] A cross-examination must ask whether we have here, notwithstanding claims to the contrary, a modern variation of the ancient Greek philosophic tendency of transposing the storyteller's references to heavenly happenings into general principles of interpreting reality — in this case a reputedly existential even if not cosmic reality — that is deemed on other grounds than the news story itself to be more in keeping with the way things are. In short, has an existential ontology, or presupposed way of being who we are, set preconditions upon what is to be heard in the Gospel's apocalyptic message? Such questioning is behind still further attempts in twentieth-century theology to differentiate the significance of biblical testimonies regarding heaven from that of myth, as well as from a univocal literalism.

3. Hearing of Heaven as Saga

Karl Barth became the major theological voice calling for a third option. In the extensive attention given to biblical testimonies regarding heaven in his *Church Dogmatics*, Barth proposes the designation of "saga" (sometimes coupled with "legend") as an alternative both to taking the biblical news of heaven literalistically, as historical fact in a univocal sense, and to taking it as myth to be demythologized. ". . . The concept of saga," Barth writes, "has to be marked off from that of myth as well as 'history.'"[52] The translator's quotation marks around 'history' in this sentence indicate that Barth writes of "history" in two senses. In this context he means verifiable world history, as when we refer to historical facts [*Historie*]. In other contexts, as we shall see, he writes of saga conveying its own "history," by which he means special occurrences [*Geschichte*].

Why is this so? Such an alternative is needed, in Barth's judgment, because both literally factual and demythologized interpretations, for all their differences, translate the news of heaven into idioms that do not rely upon the new reality of heaven's coming for their meaning. In one case, the idiom is world history in which only events that take place in a similar or univocally analogous way, as Troeltsch emphasized, are said to qualify as really happening. To this construal Barth objects that "the linguistic usage of Holy Scripture" considered in its canonical context does not draw the significance of heaven from "the known analogies of world history."[53] In the other case, the idiom is a theory of existence referred to by philosophers more technically as an existential phenomenology or ontology. To this construal as practiced in demythologization, Barth's objection is that canonical linguistic usage does not draw the significance of heaven from any redescriptions into generalities applicable to either cosmological *or* existential phenomena, "the natural and spiritual cosmos," as he puts it.[54]

"Only occurrences within the existent reality of nature can be historical," he writes. "But at this point we have to do with occurrences on the frontier of the non-existence and existence of nature. If there can be any accounts of such occurrences at all, they certainly cannot be 'historical.'"[55] When the Bible speaks of heaven and earth being created, and heaven coming to earth as a *basileia* with an accompanying media of angels, we hear of actual events that have to do, as history does, with time and space occurrences, yet not with factual events detectable as occurrences in keeping with the measurements of the natural order. Yet myth is an unsatisfactory alternative, Barth argues, for conveying what is newsworthy about these "occurrences on the frontier" of natural existence and non-existence, whether it be the existence of the cosmos at large or our more personal existence, because it lacks the concreteness of news events that actually make history. In sum, myths turn history-making news into generalizations of what is already the case. Both the univocally historical and the mythical attempts at translation finally come down to interpreting the biblical news of heaven's coming to pass, in the accounts of creation and new creation, in terms, as we have noted, of what Paul calls "the form of this world [that] is passing away." In each case the news is lost in translation. Thus Barth concludes, "It cannot be a question of translating the saga or legend into verifiable history [*Historie*], but of repeating (in whatever language) the saga or legend as such, of a renewal of the form commensurate with the history [*Geschichte*] envisaged in these accounts."[56] Note here the two senses of "history."

In sum, most simply put, "saga" is thus Barth's preferred label for differentiating the linguistic form that he finds to be most commensurate with the occurrences envisaged in the biblical accounts of heaven. That these accounts tell of specific events uniquely enacted and taking place — and not general ideas of the sort that can be extracted from a myth or fairy tale as "the moral of the story" — makes them sound like history. But insofar as the events reported, whether they be in the creation accounts, or in the Gospel proclamation of a coming *basileia* from heaven, are depicted as enacted prior to, or as having priority over, the rest of creaturely occurrences, they do not qualify as verifiably real within the boundaries of world history or natural science. For these reasons Barth refers to what biblical saga expresses as "pre-historical reality of history."[57] Franz Overbeck had earlier distinguished between a primal history (*Urgeschichte*) in the Gospel message that was not equatable with what counts today as world history (*Weltgeschichte*), but Barth's view of saga attributes more narrative content to this *Urgeschichte*. In fact, he writes that "almost the whole of the biblical history is engaged in that transition to saga or legend, and the angels in particular can only make this clear." "This does not mean," he immediately adds, "that we are in the sphere of Red Riding Hood and her grandmother and the wolf, or the stork which leaves babies, or the March hare and Father Christmas."[58] Saga's kind of once-for-all significance only arises from continually following, or adhering to, the particularities of biblical testimony without transposing its native semiotic usage and reference into an extratextual idiom. Unlike myth or fairytale as Barth views them, the point of saga, its content, is not severable from its form. In this respect, its similarity with the third definition of "literal" as the meaning that a text or discourse communicates within the context or frame of reference that is native to it, as previously mentioned, becomes apparent.

Since the German word *Geschichte* can be translated in English either as "history" or as "story," subsequent theological assessments in English have mostly discussed the kind of significance Barth designates as saga by using instead the expressions "history-like story" or "realistic narrative." Most influential in this regard has been the work of Hans Frei. Frei's study of biblical interpretation and the way in which narratives may be said to "render the identity" of their subjects appeals to critical literary theory and focuses upon recovering the "literal" meaning of texts in the third intratextual sense noted of "literal."[59] While his insights are directed primarily toward addressing identity descriptions of Jesus Christ, and not the subject of heaven, Frei's critique of myth, as well as of univocal literalism, parallels closely that of Barth.[60]

For example, consistent with his definition of saga is Barth's contention in another part of his *Church Dogmatics* that in hearing of Jesus' victory over evil we cannot grasp the person of Jesus, or indeed any person, in "the sense of conceptual apprehension and control," or as "a logical principle of grace and its triumph." Rather, "To say 'Jesus' is necessarily to say 'history [*Geschichte*]' . . ." Barth makes it clear that he does not intend in this instance verifiable world history but rather, "His history, the history in which He is what He is and does what He does."[61] This is a characteristic Barthian statement. Translate *Geschichte* here as "story," specifically "life-story," and we have in capsule Frei's keynote theme of a realistic narrative rendering the identity of its subject. The statement would then read, "To say 'Jesus' is necessarily to say 'life-story,' His life-story, the life-story in which He is what He is and does what He does." A subject whose significance only becomes known by following what happens with this subject requires narration. In such a situation a narrative provides an identity depiction that is not susceptible to paraphrase or redescription in other terms. Whether it be in the case of a realistic novel or the Bible, the story brings the subject to realization and constitutes its meaning intratextually through its plot in a manner that is different from the kind of extratextual referencing provided by either factual history or myth. Frei writes, "It is not going too far to say that the story is the meaning, or, alternatively, that the meaning emerges from the story form, rather than being merely illustrated by it, as would be the case in allegory and in a different way, in myth."[62]

If we test this option of saga or history-like realistic narrative with respect to the hearing of heaven recorded in Chapter 1, a primary insight emerges that there may be said to be a significance to the Gospel news of heaven that is enacted by this news and not extracted from it. Heaven's coming to pass in this way of hearing makes no appeal for its meaning or truth to any form of this world that the Gospel proclaims to be passing away. It follows from this proposal that the creation stories are not to be taken as scientific accounts of the origin of the universe, and the coming of the kingdom from heaven that is announced as being at hand in our midst is not a factual datum of world history. But neither do such testimonies simply transcribe experiential states of consciousness. A cross-examination must ask if this concentration upon the narrative character of this news entails that the only trustworthiness in the Gospel testimony of heaven, or its only truthfulness, is finally to be acknowledged as fictional. Does the "form commensurate with the *Geschichte* envisaged in these accounts," as Barth puts it, disallow more than only narrative significance?[63]

This brings us to a fourth major appraisal of the dogmatic significance of apocalyptic testimony that we find in the trajectory of responses prominently argued by the end of the twentieth century. It is the hearing of heaven as promise.

4. *Hearing of Heaven as Promise*

The mid-1960s saw the emergence of a provocative new theology of hope that placed a primary focus upon the promissory significance of the Bible's apocalyptic and eschatological testimonies. Of the theologians associated with this movement, the most widely read and discussed has been Jürgen Moltmann, whose two works, *Theology of Hope: On the Grounds and the Implications of a Christian Eschatology* and "Theology as Eschatology," a paper delivered at Duke University in April 1968, inaugurated one of the most ecumenical and international theological discussions of the rest of the century.[64] In a number of subsequent books Moltmann has elaborated and expanded his basic themes to address the major Christian doctrines, but the claims specifically pertaining to promissory significance that aroused the most controversy were first advanced in his initial writings.[65]

Foremost among these contested claims is the assertion that what faith hears as the Word of God in the Bible is news of a coming future that does not correspond to present experience. Both the historically factual and existential frameworks of interpretation, Moltmann argues, prove inadequate to refer to such a coming. As we find in the resurrection accounts of Jesus, this news, Moltmann writes, is indeed reported in the "form of narrative," but it is narrative in which "the modern distinction between factual truth and existential truth" is foreign.[66] "Positivistic historicism reduces history to realities that can be dated and localized, without noticing the realm of future possibilities that surrounds these realities . . . The existentialist interpretation on the other hand seeks the existential possibilities attaching to past existence in order to repeat and re-echo them . . ." What is needed, Moltmann contends, is a recognition that goes "beyond both historicism and existentialism" in acknowledging in these Gospel narratives their "significance for the future." This significance occurs when the Gospel stories in telling of Jesus risen and ascended into heaven "from whence he shall come," as the Apostles' Creed affirms it, are heard, not as stories of times past, nor as existential descriptions illustrative of present experiences, nor as historical predictions of the future, but rather as God's promises. "In this sense the event of the raising of Christ from the dead is an event which is understood only in the *modus* of promise" with its time "still ahead of it."[67]

Promise as a subject of hermeneutical inquiry can be traced throughout the history of Christian thought, and the modern debates reflect their historical antecedents. Its importance received classic statement in the words of the reformer Philip Melanchthon in 1555: "Faith does not mean merely knowing the story of Christ . . . [it] includes not only the story but also the promises and the fruit of the promise."[68] Moltmann extends the scope of Melanchthon's statement beyond simply the promise of individual forgiveness and the fruits worthy of repentance to indicate more comprehensively what he sees to be the key significance of scriptural testimony to the God who, as introduced in the book of Revelation, not only "was and is" but "is *to come*" (Rev. 1.4). In this apocalyptic context of usage the concluding words testifying of Jesus from heaven are, "Surely, I am coming soon," to which the response is given, "Amen. Come, Lord Jesus!" (Rev. 22.20). Such testimony Moltmann finds paradigmatic of a larger canonical witness of both the Old and New Testaments.[69]

In sum, to hear of this coming from heaven as God's promise, according to Moltmann's assessment, affords a different way of thinking about both the future and the present from one that takes the Gospel talk literally in a univocal historical sense, or takes it as myth to be existentially demythologized, or takes it as saga when only its narrativity or story form is brought into account. Most notably, a promised future differs from a predicted future in that a promise carries a commitment while a prediction does not.

Much of the initial reaction to Moltmann's position, especially in the United States, in retrospect can be seen to have come from a misunderstanding or rejection of what he meant by the "future."[70] The usual association the word brings to mind is of something not present. Thus, by referring to "the future as mode of God's being" Moltmann prompted the accusation among some critics that he was negating God's presence and denying the validity of present experience. He responded that, to the contrary, the eschatological character of biblical testimony conveys a different sense of the future, one more aptly conceived as *adventus* than as *futurum*. This is the decisive point.

Futurum, like its corresponding Greek root *phyo*, from which we derive our English word "physics," denotes the idea of a becoming that emerges from the potentialities of the past. An eschatological and apocalyptic sense of the future, in contrast, is of an *advent* in which a new reality comes into the present that is not accounted for as an extrapolation from any available residue of what has gone before. In the prophecy of *Isaiah* the words of God's promise are, "Do not remember the former things, or consider the things of old. I am about to do a new thing; now it springs forth, do you not perceive it" (Isa. 43.19)? The "idle tale" of the women at the tomb on Resurrection morning provides a primary New Testament example: "Why do you look for the living among the dead" (Lk. 24.5, 11)? "The authority of 'the Word,'" Moltmann writes, "proves itself first of all in that it becomes the author of new possibilities in reality. This has nothing to do with traditionalism, biblicism, or clericalism and its authoritarian understanding of the Word. But it also has nothing to do with religious liberalism for which 'the Word' of Christian proclamation is a merely symbolic expression for already available experiences."[71]

Understood as *adventus*, it is the promised future that ultimately determines what becomes of the past and present, and not the other way around, as the idea of *futurum* implies, with all prospects for what will become of things considered to be determined by their past. The prophesied Day of the Lord is characteristically proclaimed as coming from ahead, not from behind. The trajectory of its coming is not from the past into the present but from the future into the present. Biblical prophecy recalls past events as a "memory of the future"[72] in which Lot's wife is depicted as misdirected in looking back rather than forward to the Promised Land (Gen. 19.26, Lk. 17.32). What "was and is" is revealed by what is "to come."

To hear this word of heaven's coming as God's promise changes not only the way the future is perceived, Moltmann emphasizes, but even more importantly and as a consequence, the way the present is engaged. By not finding its corresponding reality in present experience, the language of promise, as Moltmann puts it, creates the experience of history. The reason this is so is that a promise creates a new reality in the present by instituting a relationship to the future that would not otherwise be the case. In the terminology of the linguistic philosophers, a promise has *performative* and not simply *informative* force in that it constitutes a commitment. Its truth can only be proven in coming events as the word of commitment is not only given but also kept and revealed to be trustworthy in what comes to pass. In the terminology of scripture, to cite words from Paul, the experience of history Moltmann describes is the sharing in "the sufferings of this present time" of a promised "glory about to be revealed" (Rom. 8.18).

It is the glory of what is promised to be that creates the engagement, and not the evasion, of the sufferings of the present. The heavenly future proves true only with reference to what is currently happening on earth. This is strikingly emphasized in the Gospel of Matthew, where the coming of the Son of Man with the glory of all the angels is promised in Jesus' teaching to be revealed precisely in the treatment of those who are currently being considered "the least" (Mt. 25.40, 45). Equally, in the Letter to the Hebrews, where much is written of a faithful hearing of the promise of heaven, it is notable that the "desire [for] a heavenly country" (Heb. 11.16) is not associated with any disregard of earth and its sufferings, but rather is depicted as a persevering on this very way of the Cross, by currently showing hospitality to strangers, and remembering those who are in prison, as though in prison with them, and those being tortured, as though being tortured as well (Heb.13.1-3).

Living by the promise of what is coming in this Gospel frame of reference, Moltmann concludes, represents no utopian evasion of present reality in favor of some never-never land of bliss beyond the sunset because it is only in relation to events happening here and now, in the social and political, as well as existential experience of history, that the promised *advent* proves to be a countervailing reality to its crucifying opposition. In doing so it reveals the constancy of the future's commitment to the present, an historical faithfulness not realized in factually demonstrable or existentialist phenomena, but in the existence of perseverance in hope *en route* to the Promised Land.

Cross-examination of this theological alternative has tended to question the adequacy of its political ethic by asking how human action is involved and may be said to bear responsibility for this coming of the future. This occurs first with the responses of the Liberation theologians, who acknowledge Moltmann's eschatological insights but call for a more concrete engagement with societal oppression, and later with the ecologically minded social ethicists, whose stress is upon a panentheistic *immanence* of "the real world" as an interdependent causal system rather than upon the alleged *imminence* of its *adventus*. Moltmann's subsequent writings have in turn responded affirmatively to the concerns of each while seeking with varying modifications to maintain the promissory significance articulated in his earlier work.

"What then Are We to Say to These Things?"

This review of four ways of regarding the significance of biblical references to heaven has intentionally focused upon theological positions responsive, both positively and negatively, to the inheritance of Johannes Weiss, Albert Schweitzer, Franz Overbeck, and other definers of what Weiss called the "modern Protestant world-view." The justification for focusing upon this particular trajectory of proposals is that the issues they address are not limited to the confines of twentieth century European Protestant theology, nor is Weiss's so-called "modern Protestant world-view" an outlook that is found only among Protestants. Whatever new theological appraisals of the biblical news of heaven are undertaken by the women and men working in today's comparatively more multi-voiced, ecumenical, interfaith, and culturally diverse contexts will, to some degree, inevitably represent critical *re*appraisals of this body of witness. It is formative insofar as its ideas further enable our own questioning about what we hear of heaven, but not normative in the sense of conclusive.

Readers who care about the subject of heaven but are less engaged with the technicalities of academic theology's recent history have every right now to ask what is gained from the foregoing review as far as how hearing the Gospel news of heaven today may be said to matter.

Two judgments at least appear to be warranted. First, the "big mistake" in the modern charge of the Gospel's false expectations regarding the coming of heaven can be seen to lie in its supposing that the news of this coming refers to the end of "the real world" rather than to its beginning. And second, what is taken to be "the real world" is shown to differ consequentially according to how the Gospel talk of heaven is heard.

On the first point, the issue of the delay of the *Parousia*, or the coming of Christ's heavenly *basileia*, is certainly indicated in some New Testament passages with Luke-Acts, for example, generally recognized as portraying this coming as less immediate than the Gospel of Mark. Yet in both the Lucan and Marcan accounts a consistent prohibition is equally emphasized against accounting for any true arrival from heaven as a matter of a timetable prediction: "It is not good for you to know the times or periods that the Father has set by his own authority" (Acts 1.7); "But about that day or hour no one knows, neither the angels of heaven, nor the Son, but only the Father" (Mk. 13.32, cf. Mt. 24.36); and, "Beware, keep alert; for you do not know when the time will come" (Mk. 13.33). Similarly, in the writings of First and Second Peter, where "the end of all things" is also said to be "near at hand" (1 Pet. 4.7), those who scoff at the delay of waiting for the promised new heavens and a new earth are reminded that "with the Lord one day is like a thousand years, and a thousand years are like one day" (2 Pet. 3.8).

Only by a univocally literalistic hearing can the charge be sustained that news of a kingdom now coming from heaven to counter the form of this world that is passing away lacks trustworthy credibility. Rather, it now more plainly appears that the late nineteenth-century optimism expressed in Weiss's statement that "we pass our lives in the joyful confidence that *this* world will evermore become the showplace of the people of God" displays an unrealistic and untrustworthy credulity on the part of such a "modern Protestant world-view." It fails to take account of the apocalyptic distinction, rightly recognized but wrongly evaluated by Weiss, between what is said to be coming to pass from heaven and what is said to be passing away as the form of this world and merely assumes the same reality status of each. *Only when one thinks of the fulfillment of what is coming to pass according to the measurements applicable to what Paul calls the schema or form of this world that is passing away can one speak of the Gospel as obviously mistaken in its imminent expectations.* At the least, we may conclude that it is not so simplistically arguable that the early church got the news of heaven wrong and Christian faith has had to make allowances for this mistake ever since.

As to the second point, the insight to be gained from the foregoing summary analysis of different ways the Gospel talk of heaven may be taken serves to counteract a closed mind-set that tends to block hearing anything of heaven today as news. Countering such foreclosure of thinking about "the real world" is what the hearing of heaven is all about. With no other subject is the opposition to the foreclosure of what we take to be real more pronounced.

The theological accounts of the ways of literalism, myth, saga, and promise in responding to the news of heaven do not in themselves have the power to make this news significant to any of us as a matter of real-life importance. Each answers some questions and leaves others still to be more adequately addressed. Notwithstanding this inconclusiveness, by attending to them we are enabled to see why such real-life importance cannot creditably be dismissed or simply ruled to be impossible at the present time. This is no minor gain. Clearing away the growth of conventional underbrush serves a critical function in allowing for the recognition of things otherwise obscured. Such may be the case with respect to conventions of modern thought insofar as they erroneously take for granted that the only options for making current sense of the biblical news of heaven would be to treat it as empirically verifiable, as objectively cosmological, as existentially or morally anthropological, or as a social construction of reality. On the other hand, merely proposing as counterpoints the labels "eschatological" or "apocalyptic" does not in itself provide an account for the hope of heaven either. Theological clearing is a necessary, even if not alone a sufficient, step in dogmatics. Cynicism is shown to be as unwarranted and untrustworthy as credulity.

This realization runs through the forty years of correspondence between Bultmann and Barth, with their mutual opposition to a univocal literalism and yet their frustrating inability to reach agreement, or make sure they even understand each other, regarding myth, and saga, and promise. "The decisive thing," Bultmann writes Barth in one of their most earnest exchanges, "is to make clear with what concept of reality, of being and events, we really operate in theology, and how this relates to the concepts in which not only other people think and speak of reality, being, and events, but in which we theologians also think and speak in our everyday lives."[73] To this "decisive thing" and the challenge it poses, Chapter 3 will be directed.

Chapter 3

THE REALITY OF HEAVEN

A recurring expression in these pages up to this point has been "the real world." For the most part I have put it in quotation marks to emphasize that it is the colloquial usage which I wish to highlight and also that this usage, despite its vernacular familiarity, has no commonly recognized referent. We do speak of "the real world" and argue about what positions are and are not realistic. Quite often the words serve as an epithet directed against those being charged with the naiveté or self-delusion of, as we say, "*not* living in the real world." Critics of the illusory character of much heaven talk — Feuerbach, Nietzsche, Marx, and Freud being the prime influencers in modern Western thought — variously emphasize the extent to which such talk reflects the projection of our repressions, both psychological and societal. They point to its debilitating function of undercutting human responsibility. Yet the dispellers of illusion do not themselves escape being charged with it as other contexts and frames of reference are brought into consideration. Despite its ambiguity, the "real world" is supposed today from various angles of vision in more than one way. A most unlikely supposition may be heard in the Gospel testimony that tells of a heavenly coming of life now at hand. What case can be made for hearing of this heavenly coming as having to do with the reality in our everyday lives is the question Bultmann presses upon Barth in their correspondence in 1952.[1] This is the question now before us in Chapter 3.

In the twentieth-century legacy of responses to Weiss, Schweitzer, and Overbeck on the Gospel news of the at-handedness of God's kingdom from heaven that we have just considered, we find that both the advocates of myth and of saga from their different perspectives underscore the difficulty of accounting for the "real-world" significance of the news of heaven. Paul Tillich wrote of the mythic symbol of a coming kingdom of heaven as "most important and most difficult for Christian thought" and lamented its loss of vitality in the history of modern Christianity.[2] For his part, Karl Barth began his discussion of the role of saga in addressing what he titled "The Kingdom of Heaven, The Ambassadors of God and Their Opponents" by acknowledging at the outset that on the subject of heaven's coming and the angels "there has always been a good deal of theological caprice, of valueless, grotesque and even absurd speculation, and also of no less doubtful skepticism," and by commenting that "the dogmatic sphere which we have to enter and traverse in this section is the most remarkable and difficult of all."[3] Remarkable indeed is the fact that after first declaring heaven to be inconceivable, incomparable, unimaginable, inaccessible, and indescribable, Barth then proceeds to devote more than four hundred pages to explaining its reality![4] We have noted as well that Moltmann's proposal of promise for its part also initially met with critical questions regarding its adequacy for addressing the experience of present-day reality and its societal engagement.

Why not, it may be wondered, simply posit heaven as a "spiritual reality" and just leave it at that?[5] To which, of course, one obvious answer is, because the Bible itself, if that is the Gospel news one is hearing, does not just "leave it at that" in referring to "the mysteries of the kingdom of heaven" (Mt. 13.11). Yet if such Gospel depictions do not conform to the terms, as Barth puts it, of any "real factors" of the world that are empirically verifiable, or objectively cosmological, or subjectively anthropological, or a social construction, what sense does it make today, if any, to speak of heaven as reality?

It was from this mid-twentieth century context of deliberation that Rudolf Bultmann pressed the reality question with Barth, whose claims for saga in articulating the "real-world" significance of heaven led to his calling for nothing less than a radical redefinition of what Bultmann had first proposed as the task of demythologization. Barth's case for this redefining of demythologization introduces two terms not customarily associated with Barthian theology: "imagination" and "disbelief." In this chapter we will turn our attention to Barth's particular use of these two terms by first taking note of the New Testament background regarding the role of parable and of apocalyptic testimony in expressing the news of a heavenly inbreaking, and then by asking how Barth's account, now over a half-century later, finds resonance, in Bultmann's words, with how "other people think and speak of reality, being, and events" in everyday life today.

No theologian of the twentieth century has bequeathed to us such detailed attention to the import of the biblical news of heaven in its various facets than has Karl Barth. For this reason, Barth's legacy, regardless of any agreement or disagreement we may have with it, provides a logical place to pursue our specific inquiry. Furthermore, no twentieth-century thinker on the subject of heaven's at-handedness can be said to have left us with a more unhesitating provocation. To the argument that the Gospel message is plainly mistaken in its imminent expectations — because thinking univocally of the fulfillment of what is coming to pass according to the measurements applicable to what Paul calls the *schema* or form of this world that is passing away allegedly shows it to be so — Barth's cryptic comment delivers the *coup de grâce*: "the categorical assertion that this expectation of something at hand 'was not fulfilled' is too obvious to be convincing"[6]

"And Through a Riddle, at the Last . . ."

"*Too obvious to be convincing*!" After following this trajectory of modern theological responses since Weiss, are we led back again at the last to the poetic promptings of Emily Dickinson?

> And through a Riddle, at the last —
> Sagacity, must go —

If so, it is to a deeper sense of "riddle" than we (but perhaps not she!) may initially have realized. What definitely cannot be described as "obvious," either to its earliest hearers or today, is the way the Gospel news of a heavenly kingdom is conveyed. In the reported teaching of Jesus in the Synoptic Gospel texts, such a heavenly state of affairs *at* hand, but not *in* hand, is said to be conveyed through *parable*. Matthew's Gospel states, "Jesus told the crowds all these things in parables; without a parable he told them nothing" (Mt. 13.34). Again, "This is why I speak to them in parables, because seeing they do not see, and hearing they do not hear, nor do they understand" (Mt. 13.13). The textual witness as well of Mark and of Luke on the role of parable is consistent. In the Pauline texts, where expressions of *apocalypse* are more characteristic than *parable* in referring to what is "at hand" and "taking place,"[7] and in the Gospel of John as well, we still also hear of listeners pointed to a significance in familiar situations of their day, not publicly observable as signs of heaven according to the listeners' prevailing perceptions.

The Pauline scholar J. Louis Martyn has described Paul's message of the Gospel in his Letter to the Galatians as follows:

In short, it is not as though, provided with a good religious foundation for a good religious ladder, one could ascend from the wrong to the right. Things are the other way around. God has elected to invade the realm of the wrong — "the present evil age" (1.4) — by sending God's Son and the Spirit of the Son into it from outside it (4.4-6). And it is in this apocalyptic invasion that God has liberated us from the powers of the present evil age . . . Galatians is a particularly clear witness to one of Paul's basic convictions: the gospel is not about human movement into blessedness (religion); it is about God's liberating invasion of the cosmos . . ."[8]

To reiterate what we have previously noted in Chapter 1, the *basileia's* coming is said not to be subject to public observation; "not coming with signs to be observed," as Luke's Gospel expresses it. When in our midst it does not lend itself, we are told, to anyone's saying, "It's here," or, "It's there" (Lk. 17.20-21). Paul, for his part, writes that "flesh and blood cannot inherit" this *basileia*, any more than can that which is perishable and passing away be said to inherit, or be endowed with, what is imperishable and coming to pass (1 Cor. 15.50). In short, to repeat once again the Fourth Gospel's account of the words of Jesus, "My *basileia* is not of [or from] this world (ἐκ τοῦ κόσμου)" (Jn 18.36).

If we now take the import of the kingdom parables in the Synoptic Gospels to be "apocalyptic" — in this precise sense of conveying an incalculable cosmic inbreaking — we must distinguish this function of parable from one that simply denotes some obvious moral of a story that merely tells its hearers what they otherwise already know. The parabolic significance of the "riddle" posed by news of heaven as a *basileia* that comes to us in this world, but not as part of this world, does not conform to prior conditions. To be sure, in the parables of the heavenly *basileia's* forthcoming in the Synoptic texts the imminence of heaven is said to be *like* such ordinary, this-earthly realities as a sower of seed, a grain of mustard seed when it is sowed, leaven in bread, treasure hidden in a field, a merchant seeking pearls, a fishing net, a king seeking to settle accounts, a householder hiring laborers, a royal host inviting guests to a wedding feast, or ten bridesmaids with their lamps going at night to meet the bridegroom.[9] But these current likenesses to what is at hand are said to provide no obvious conformity to heaven's coming as if it were an immanent event. What is imminent is not immanent. Parables of the kingdom, so we hear reported of Jesus as he draws near to Jerusalem, are told to signify to their listeners what is other than their current suppositions and not immediately apparent (Lk. 19.11).

Twentieth-century textual scholarship regarding these parables of the kingdom since Weiss and Schweitzer generally follows a preference for what Ernst Troeltsch called a "historical" rather than a "dogmatic" accounting and takes a form-critical approach in concentrating primarily upon the originating context.[10] Where it has not done so, interpreters have risked being accused of reading too much of the present back into the past. A much acclaimed work of the 1950s by Joachim Jeremias, *The Parables of Jesus*, for example, comes to be criticized in the 1980s for having interpreted the significance of the synoptic texts of Jesus' parables too much in Bultmannian and modern existentialist terms.[11] In a similar vein, still later criticism of a postmodernist persuasion has characterized the entire leading line of historical interpretations of Jesus' teaching, with all their diversity, from C. H. Dodd's *The Parables of the Kingdom* in the 1930s to John Dominic Crossan's *In Parables: The Challenge of the Historical Jesus* in the 1990s, as demonstrating that "the model used to interpret Jesus the parabler, more often than not, is a contemporary one."[12]

Whatever the bias for, or against, historical versus dogmatic interpretations (and the labels have been further refined since Troeltsch's day), most New Testament interpreters of the Gospel parables today are forced to admit that the two perspectives cannot be completely separated. This is especially the case if we are to speak of parabolic *significance* since, by agreed definition, to hear a parable is to hear it in what are to the hearer current, everyday terms. Parabolic significance involves the use of terms familiar to the hearer to signify what is unfamiliar to the hearer. On this the historical–critical interpreters are agreed. "Significance beyond what is immediately evident from the everyday meaning of the words," is the way one textual interpreter of the New Testament passages puts it.[13] "Comparisons between eternal, transcendental realities and that which was familiar to the common human experience of [Jesus'] day," is the way another expresses it.[14] In short, "The earthly picture has a heavenly meaning," writes a third.[15]

With specific regard to hearing the apocalyptic news of heaven, a parabolically significant situation is further said by parable scholars to be one where there is an awareness that what is evidently passing away is somehow subject to what is not yet evidently coming to pass. John Drury writes of "the intervening tension being the experience of the reader or hearer in an age quickly passing away but concealing in itself and its dying the age to come. It is in this intervening phase that the parable belongs and from which it looks back and forward over the whole range of history from start to finish."[16] With respect to the entrenched powers of such an age, parables are said to function as "subversive speech."[17] Existence in such a situation, to borrow a phrase that has been used to characterize Paul's apocalyptic theology of the Cross, is life "at the turn of the ages."[18]

Discernment of what is really happening at the present time is closely associated in traditions of Gospel testimonies with the significance of parables. It is noteworthy how often in these testimonies the emphasis falls upon noticing, or the failure to notice, what is currently taking place. In this respect, knowing what time it is intersects with the rhetoric about who is, or who is not, facing the reality now impending in their midst. Noticing is the whole point of the Gospel parables: "Let anyone with ears to hear listen!" (Mt. 13.9, Mk. 4.9, Lk. 8.8). To the disciples this question is put, "Do you have eyes, and fail to see? Do you have ears, and fail to hear?" (Mk. 8.18). Luke records Jesus' rebuke of those who know how to forecast the weather but do not know how to interpret the present time (Lk. 12.54-56). Similarly, in the account of the final entry into Jerusalem, the word of Jesus as reported is, ". . . You did not know the time of your visitation" (Lk. 19.44).

The Lesson of the Fig Tree

A striking example of the way in which Gospel testimonies may be heard to juxtapose the familiar with the unfamiliar in telling what time it is occurs in two brief scriptural passages having to do with the lesson of the fig tree.

In one instance that speaks of what is coming from heaven — the coming Son of man in Mark's and Matthew's texts, the coming *basileia* of God in Luke's version — we hear these words that Jesus is said to speak to his disciples in parable:

> From the fig tree learn its lesson: as soon as its branch becomes tender and puts forth its leaves, you know that summer is near. So also, when you see these things taking place, you know that he (or it) is near, at the very gates (Mk. 13.28-29; cf. Mt. 24.32-33 and Lk.21.29-31).

The "lesson" to be learned would seem to be that the natural sequence of the seasons evidenced in the fig tree's sprouting of new leaves, a familiar sight in the vicinity of the Gospel's original hearers, tells the true time of heaven's coming. That which is close by, or proximate, the fig tree, has a lesson to teach the disciples by serving as a familiar indication to them of what is at hand.

By comparison, we have an earlier account in the Gospels of Mark and Matthew (there is no parallel in Luke) of Jesus and the twelve disciples with a fig tree:

On the following day, when they came from Bethany, he was hungry. Seeing in the distance a fig tree in leaf, he went to see whether perhaps he would find anything on it. When he came to it, he found nothing but leaves, for it was not the season for figs. He said to it, "May no one ever eat fruit from you again ." And his disciples heard it. (Matthew adds, "And the fig tree withered at once.") (Mk. 11.12-14; cf. Mt. 21.18-19).

The seeming injustice here to the fig tree for being blamed by Jesus when it was not in season to bear fruit provoked Bertrand Russell's satirical criticism in speaking before the National Secular Society of London in 1927 on "Why I Am Not A Christian:" "This is a very curious story," Russell observed to his free-thinking audience, "because it was not the right time of the year for figs, and you really could not blame the tree. I cannot myself feel that either in the manner of wisdom or in the matter of virtue Christ stands quite as high as some other people known to history."[19] With his low tolerance for what he took to be biblical nonsense, Russell also, of course, had nothing good to say about the Gospel talk of heaven either and concluded that the only future worth trusting from seeing "the world as it is," as he put it, is the future that "our intelligence can create."[20] Such was the lesson, in his hearing, of the fig tree.

My purpose is not to suggest that there is only one way these passages may be heard, or only one lesson to be drawn. A comprehensive textual exegesis is not the intent. Rather, the point is to observe how matters that are familiar and proximate to the disciples, in this case a fig tree and its seasons, become juxtaposed in the Gospel message with matters unfamiliar and incapable of prior approximation that are associated with a coming from heaven — in the first instance, a coming of "the Son of man," or the "*basileia* of God," and in the second instance, a coming upon the scene of Jesus himself. The familiarity with "leaves appearing on the branch" provides a foretelling of the summer that is coming in due season. Parables begin with images that are proximate to the hearers and familiar. But Christ's coming to the fig tree turns out not to approximate or fit the fig tree's familiar season. Bertrand Russell's observation that "it was not the right time of the year for figs" was only superficially correct, according to the Gospel accounts. It misses the deeper significance that the "right time" is reset, as it were, in a parabolic hearing by what comes from heaven and recreates what the due season is. It follows from this significance that the lesson of the fig tree is an awareness that what is evidently passing away is somehow subject to what is not yet evidently coming to pass. It has to do, in the words once again of John Drury, with "an age quickly passing away but concealing in itself and its dying the age to come." In the world of such Gospel parables whatever is not ready at heaven's coming proves fruitless. Put more consistently with the positive way that the Gospel proclaims it, the good news of the fig tree is in hearing that "the right time" of our lives is set by the realization of the new life that is in season with what is currently arriving on the scene from heaven.

How then do Barth's dogmatic claims regarding heaven's "reality" compare with this background of New Testament interpretation?

"Divinatory Imagination" and "Faithful Disbelief": Barth

The origins of Barth's redefining of "demythologization" we have seen in the way in which he differentiates negatively the biblical news of heaven as "saga" from both a verifiable reporting of factual history and from what Bultmann and Tillich interpret to be existential myth.

Put positively, he argues in an extended commentary on the biblical testimony that saga conveys heaven's real-world significance by involving what he calls "divinatory imagination" (*divinatorischen Phantasie*) and "an act of the unbelief which is grounded in faith" (*ein Akt des im Glauben begründeten Unglaubens sein*), or, more simply translated, "faithful disbelief."[21] Barth's reality claims for heaven that lead to his redefining of demythologization are developed with respect to these two terms. What, we may now ask, is his contention?

To appeal to imagination and disbelief in this connection seems at first hearing a most unlikely approach since one would assume that the whole point of claiming that heaven is real is to make it less imaginary and more believable. If we follow Barth's line of argument, however, it proves to be in keeping with what may be called parabolic significance and yet introduces a crucial dimension to the subject that parabolic interpretation based only upon historical–critical textual interpretation has often failed to take into account.[22]

Barth employs the term "saga" in two ways. By it he designates in the first instance one linguistic form of expression found alongside such other discursive forms ingredient in the literature of the Bible as, to cite his examples, "address, doctrine, meditation, law, epigram, epic and lyric," as well as "history," "fairytale," and "myth."[23] Secondly, as previously mentioned in Chapter 2, he uses the word more comprehensively in writing of the kind of meaning, or significance, that is most congruent with a faithful hearing of the biblical testimony as a whole: "For in some way, we repeat, almost the whole of the biblical history is engaged in that transition to saga or legend, and the angels in particular can only make this clear."[24] In each instance a poetic envisioning by divinatory imagination, a way of seeing what is going on, that allows for more actuality than factuality is said to be characteristic of saga, both in it origins and in its current hearing.

By the term "divinatory imagination" Barth characterizes biblical saga regarding heaven as employing "the freer observation and speech of poetry" in recounting history-making events that cannot themselves be accounted for as world history, in that time and space are portrayed as subject to them, rather than they being subject to time and space.[25] As poetic observation configures familiar imagery in evoking extraordinary vision of what is hitherto imperceptible, and, so to say, off our operative radar screens of detection, so does biblical testimony in telling of heaven's creation and of all that is depicted as new creation coming from heaven. It is only by becoming *parabolically* "likened" in this manner as, in Barth's words, "reflected in the natural relationships and processes of earth" that heaven is recognized as "real in the cosmic sense," and Barth writes that "as the kingdom of God is known or missed in these parables, heaven is also known or missed."[26] But what is at stake in such "an intuitive and poetic picture," Barth contends, is not the familiarity of the earthly likenesses themselves in their natural relationships and processes, whether ancient or modern, nor any efforts on our part to make them more so, but precisely the unfamiliarity of the history-making events they envision as not conforming to "ordinary analogies."[27] As with the self-revealing God of the Bible, such history-making events of heaven's creation and forthcoming, while parabolically likened, nevertheless "cannot be confused," Barth writes, "with any static or dynamic, spiritual or material circumstance of the created cosmos." That there is witness to world reality other than such "spiritual or material circumstance of the created cosmos," as he calls it, Barth finds biblically depicted as heavenly reality that is instantiated by the angels as heaven's "ambassadors."[28]

According to biblical testimony the actual world is created as heaven and earth. This is the cosmos that God calls into being, "the ordered and fashioned universe."[29] Heaven and earth together and not separately are envisaged as "two great distinctive but related spheres" comprising one "reality" and one "world," but not as evidenced by homogenous phenomena.[30] The latter point Barth stresses. Heaven is not represented as analogous to earth but as inconceivable and invisible in comparison. It is thus not knowable as simply a higher degree, a sort of super-earth extension, of what from an earthly perspective is considered natural, as proponents of supernaturalism mistakenly assume. Heaven is distinctive in that it is portrayed as directed toward earth, as overarching it, and as "from thence" God's initiating actions are said to come in relating to earth. Because this one world of God's creation is envisioned as two distinctive but related spheres, its cosmic reality does not conform to any general metaphysics or generic ontology premised upon a univocity of being. Hence Barth's claim is that having eyes to see and ears to hear this parabolic reality of the world involves "divinatory imagination" expressed in "the freer observation and speech of poetry" as it becomes "commensurate with the *Geschichte*" (non-univocal events) "envisaged in these (biblical) accounts."[31] As with all revelation of God, this commensurability of our knowing with God's doing is the gift of God's free grace; it is not something our hermeneutical techniques can make happen. In this respect "the real world" as God's creation and the work of God's Word and Spirit can only prove, and not be proven, to be so. But from an incarnational perspective of the "Word made flesh," the affirmation that heaven as God's creation and the course of God's forthcoming is primarily a spiritual reality does not deny that in its own distinctive way it embraces physical reality as well. From the start, Barth's incarnational opposition to any disembodied spiritualism or idealistic denial of materiality holds that "there is no Word of God without a physical event."[32] The "real world" is the eventuation of heaven in the midst of earth. This kind of happening biblical saga conveys with divinatory imagination.

As early as 1916, when he was still a pastor in a small Swiss village, we find Barth emphasizing that what we confront in biblical testimony of heaven is indeed presented as "the real world." That is, the Gospel message concerning heaven is never cast idealistically as "if only this were so." The scriptural accounts, whatever the various forms of speech that have gone into their composition, are not rendered as ideal worlds but as reality depictions. They tell of what God says and does and promises to do as that which currently is coming to pass, and takes place, "in the fullness of time," or "in due season," at the right time. What we find in the Bible when we dare to look, the young pastor Karl Barth wrote before the direction of his own life had become clear, is not primarily history, though some history is there, and not morality, though some morality is there, and not religion, though some religion is there. What we find is "a strange new world." It is "a new heaven and a new earth," Barth wrote, of a God who is heavenly, but heavenly "upon earth" and "will not allow life to be split into a 'here' and 'beyond'." It is "therefore, a new humanity, new families, new relationships, new politics. It has no respect for old traditions simply because they are traditions, for old solemnities simply because they are solemn, for old powers simply because they are powerful . . . The Holy Spirit establishes the righteousness of heaven in the midst of the unrighteousness of earth and will not stop nor stay until all that is dead has been brought to life and a new *world* has come into being. This is within the Bible."[33]

Similarly, over thirty years later in his work as a professor of dogmatics, we find Barth continuing to stress the reality theme in his *Church Dogmatics* when writing about the coming *basileia* of heaven according to the Gospel accounts.[34]

> And in coming to us, it brings heaven with it. It brings the higher world down to the lower. It is the kingdom in which the kingship of God means that the forces of what is in principle the unseen and heavenly world assume form and enter the earthly world and become active in it and *real factors in its occurrence.* (Italics are mine.)

Yet, Barth explicitly rejects any metaphysical category of "phenomenon" as inapplicable to this news of heaven's reality. In his dogmatic critique, to recognize the role of divinatory imagination in the biblical news of heaven is not to say that heaven is imaginary in a make-believe sense, or that it is the subjective product of a human faculty of imagination. Rather, he argues (quite in contrast to the conventional charge of critics who say that his theology allows no role for imagination!) that hearing of heaven from a biblical perspective involves poetic sensibility commensurate with the news itself, hence the term "divinatory imagination," or *Phantasie*, suggesting, I think it not too much of a stretch to say, an almost jazz-like resonance for improvisations of a subject that is, to recall again Dickinson's words,

> Invisible, as Music —
> But positive, as Sound —

But now, in addition, and most crucially, the parables of the heavenly *basileia's* coming are said not only to involve having ears to hear and eyes of poetic imagination to envision the proximate that cannot be approximated, they also engage their hearers in an active refusal. An engagement as well as an envisagement takes place in parabolic renderings of reality. The "real world's" occurrence as biblically envisioned,

Barth argues, elicits a refusal of all that currently opposes heaven's coming and is inimical to it, what he terms an "exorcism" of heaven's counterfeit opposition. The realizing of heaven's coming to pass, both in a noetic (state-of-mind) and cosmic (state-of-affairs) sense of coming into realization, entails a refusal to trust in what is passing away. This is the refusal that Barth calls "faithful disbelief."

By 1950 Barth may be seen to have turned the demythologization debate in a different direction. He essentially redefines Bultmann's term by arguing that a genuine demythologization in keeping with the Gospel news of heaven requires not a mere redescription or translation of this news from a cosmic into an existential happening — as if somehow such translation could make heaven more believable to the modern mind — but rather requires an active disbelief of noncompliance and refusal of allegiance toward what the Gospel exposes as the countervailing opposition to heaven's coming; that is, the enmity biblically characterized as evil and the demonic. The myth to be concerned about, Barth argues, is not an outdated cosmological imagery but a misplaced confidence in heaven's opposing counterfeit as if it were "the real world." Thus Barth concludes:[35]

> Faith in God and His angels involves demythologization in respect of the devil and demons; but not in the superficial phenomenological sense current to-day, in which they are grouped with the angels and even with God's own Word and work as the figures of a world-outlook which has now been superseded . . . The demythologization which will really hurt them as required cannot consist in questioning their existence. Theological exorcism must be an act of the disbelief (*Unglaubens*) which is grounded in faith.

That the news of the Gospel announces a deadly opposition to what comes from heaven is made plain by the message of the Crucifixion. That it also pronounces this deadly opposition to be overpowered and disenthralled of any pretense to be believed as "the real world" is made equally plain by the message of the Resurrection.

In the nineteenth century, Friedrich Schleiermacher, often considered to be the exemplar of a consciousness-centered anthropological approach in modern theology that Barth rejects, had also advocated what he termed "divinatory method" as a necessary component along with more grammatical and comparative hermeneutical approaches in the understanding of texts.[36] Despite strong differences Barth respected Schleiermacher, and a comparison of the ways they each employ the

"divinatory" term is illuminating. For Schleiermacher and his followers in the romantic tradition the focus is acknowledged to be more
psychological, concentrating on the attempt to divine the state of mind
of an author's thought process in conceiving and producing a text.
Apocalyptic texts envisioning a more cosmic state of affairs, such as
the creation of a new heaven and earth, are explicitly disregarded by
Schleiermacher in applying his hermeneutical theory of "divinatory
method" to the New Testament.[37] The divinatory task of achieving
understanding he likens to our own early learning development when
we find ourselves in situations we do not understand.[38]

> Even in what is familiar we encounter something that is unusual in
> the language, when a combination of words does not become evi-
> dent to us, when a train of thought strikes us as odd, even though
> it is analogous to our own, [or] when the connection between
> the various parts of a train of thought or its extension remains
> uncertain and hovers unsteadily before us. On such occasions, we
> can always begin with the same divinatory boldness.

How Barth's appeal to "divinatory imagination" contrasts with
Schleiermacher's "divinatory method" may best be illustrated by simply observing how the above quotation might sound in an apocalyptic
rather than an anthropological or psychological frame of reference. The
encounter in what is familiar of the unusual that is not yet "evident to
us," when a "train of thought strikes us as odd" and "hovers unsteadily
before us," as Schleiermacher expresses it, could just as aptly be said
to describe parabolically, not simply a subjective state of mind, but
an apocalyptic state of "world occurrence" that Barth finds biblically
envisaged by "divinatory imagination." Take, for example, Barth's
simple statement, "Thus heaven dawns on earth."[39] Considered only
noetically as a state of mind it is readily interpreted as the expression,
"It dawned on me," in the sense that we say of an idea, "It occurred
to me." Situated as it is, however, in a passage of his dogmatics where
Barth is emphasizing that the kingdom of heaven is "also real in the cosmic sense," the dawning of heaven referred to sounds more materially
akin to an earthly state of affairs and not only to one's mental state.

What distinguishes "the real world" in this more cosmic frame of
reference is not an earth devoid of heaven, as if to be realistic one would
have to grant that heaven were only an illusion, but rather a heaven, as
a "living space" in the midst of earth, that is devoid of the delusions of
hell — with "hell" in this instance denoting all that seeks to deny and
usurp such living space of heaven's coming. Not the illusion of heaven

as the projection of our earthly repressions, but the delusion which hell, as whatever opposes heaven's coming, fosters in the oppressions of earth is the issue at stake. In this manner Barth links his characterization of saga as involving "divinatory imagination" with the role of "faithful disbelief" and what he calls a "theological exorcism" in the face of heaven's counterfeiting opposition.

This "faithful disbelief" of hell, as heaven's opposition, is not the faithless unbelief of a so-called modern mind denying hell's existence as simply an outdated myth; on the contrary, it is a refusal to trust in what hell seeks to impose as "the real world." ". . . In the light of . . . the kingdom of God coming from heaven to earth," Barth writes, "that which contradicts and resists it, as it is driven from the field is seen much more clearly than where there is only a movement towards the fulfillment and the kingdom is only announced."[40] In other words, the *basileia* of heaven's entry into the atmosphere of earth is portrayed in the Gospel accounts as meeting with deadly resistance, a countervailing field of force. This claim of countervalence is what we have seen that Johannes Weiss judged to be no longer tenable for the modern mind to accept. Yet the reach of this deadly opposition is what the passion narratives of the Gospels relate in telling of what happens with Jesus Christ, whom the Gospel of John describes as having come "down from heaven" to do the will of the one who sent him (Jn 6.38).

Parabolically configured, "the real world," according to this construal of the Gospel's heaven testimony, is not faced simply by having eyes to see and ears to hear the unfamiliar dawning upon the familiar, the extraordinary transforming the ordinary. Nietzsche's "Platonism for the masses" could say as much. Rather, to recall again the words of Ephesians, being seated in "the heavenly places" also involves here and now an engagement of earthly struggle with "cosmic powers of this present darkness," a persevering refusal to acquiesce to the forces of evil seeking currently to usurp rule and authority in place of heaven itself (Eph. 6.12). These opposing powers, variously referred to in the scriptures as sin, Satan, the devil, the Antichrist, the beast, and the demons, are depicted as exercising a pseudo-agency that is distinctly other from the agency of the Creator and from God's good creation in the biblical drama of creation and redemption. They are the deceptive and tempting counterfeits of reality, revealed for the deadly delusions they are by the power overcoming them, having no real-world status in creation of their own and no *basileia* except one going "to destruction" (Rev. 17.8). Such would-be nullifying opponents of heaven's inbreaking, or *das Nichtige* as Barth refers to these deceptive forces,[41] have their pseudo-agency unmasked for what it is only by the actual taking-place of what they war against, the "real world" of the *basileia* from heaven that is parabolically instantiated and realized in the witness of its accompanying angels. "We know about them only in such a way that — as and because we believe in God and His angels — we oppose to them the most radical disbelief (*Unglauben*)."[42]

It follows that whatever "riddle" such a hearing poses to "sagacity," if heaven is heard of as news of a state of affairs that is apocalypsed, or takes place, in our midst "like this," as the parables say, at once proximate or close to what is currently familiar, but not approximated in conformity to our preconceptions, this parabolic significance, which includes not only envisagement but engagement in current affairs, cannot be confined only to literary or historical texts so designated by form-criticism as parables of the kingdom in the Gospels of Matthew, Mark, and Luke, or indeed to the Bible itself. Such confinement would imply either that there were no longer any news events of a heavenly *basileia* at hand — merely historical reports of such news in the past — or that God's forthcoming from heaven could be made subject to scribal encryption.

On this point Barth's own position against all parochial confinements is as unequivocal as it is remarkable. Now if we "eavesdrop in the world at large" from "the narrow corner in which we have our place and task," he writes, "we can and must be prepared to encounter 'parables of the kingdom' in the full biblical sense, not merely in the . . . works and words of the Christian Church, but also in the secular sphere . . . in the strange interruption of the secularism of life in the world (*der Profanität des Weltlebens*)."[43]

Eavesdropping on Secularity's Strange Interruptions

This call to "eavesdrop" upon the world at large from the theologian's "narrow corner" in expectation of encountering parables of the heavenly basileia *pro-fanum*, "outside the temple" in the profane life of the world, represents Barth's response to "the decisive thing," as Bultmann had urged, that theologians make clear how their talk of reality relates to reality talk found elsewhere. The question is about the relation of discourses, not about equivalence. It is telling that Barth in acknowledging secularity does not employ the term "profane" pejoratively. Having explored the Gospel significance of heaven's forthcoming as an incalculable cosmic inbreaking — both apocalyptic and parabolic in this sense — it follows that he sees the encountering of such parables of the kingdom not as conforming to the lexicon of secularity but as a "strange interruption" not amenable to its schematizations. Secular symbols do not make the Gospel news of heaven relevant. Yet Barth has said as much with respect to the lexicon of religion. Religious symbols do not make the Gospel news of heaven relevant. It is precisely the irrelevance of the Gospel news of heaven's forthcoming with respect both to the secular and religious schemata of a world said to be "passing away" which witnesses to "the real world" that is coming to pass. In everyday English speech "the profane" carries the dictionary definitions of that which is considered not sacred, not religious, not mysterious, not hallowed, but irreverent, disrespectful, and even contemptuous of sacred claims.[44] Precisely in such precincts disclaiming any adherence to the church's talk of a heavenly kingdom, faith must be prepared to encounter, Barth argues, the biblically parabolic truth of the *basileia* of heaven's reality.

In asking how such theological talk of reality relates to talk of the "real" beyond theology's narrow corner, two secular examples currently offer special instances for comparison. Both are ways of speaking that have come to prominence since Barth's day, and both, in quite different respects, defy the foreclosures on thinking of "the real world" earlier taken to be self-evident by Weiss and other definers of the so-called "modern Protestant world-view." The first example comes from the self-described "atheist" hearing of Paul's testimony to the Resurrection set forth by the French philosopher Alain Badiou in *Saint Paul: The Foundation of Universalism* (1997, 2003). "It is truly another figure of the real that is in question," Badiou writes, as he proceeds to show why the news of Christ's resurrection as declared by Paul in his epistles may be said to introduce us to "the only real of any import" (55, 58). The second, from a less academic and more popular context of usage, is the emergence of "virtual reality" talk that accompanied the age of the Internet.

1. *"The Only Real of any Import"*

Outside the ecclesial purview of Christian dogmatics, a confluence of parallel interests in the Pauline epistles since the late 1990s today finds expression in the unconventional works of such hermeneutical philosophers and social theorists as, most prominently, Jacob Taubes, Alain Badiou, Slavoj Žižek, and Giorgio Agamben.[45] To focus upon Badiou's *Saint Paul* for example, a clear distancing is asserted from any theological considerations. Badiou sweepingly disavows any "religious" interest in Paul, "for the Good News he declares, or the cult dedicated to him"(1). Despite his appropriation of Pauline terminology, it is, Badiou insists, a "wholly secularized conception of grace" that he seeks to propound (66). This insistently atheist and anti-theological

THE REALITY OF HEAVEN ❖ 67

characterization of the reality conveyed by Paul's resurrection discourse only mentions heaven once in passing, in briefly remarking that "hell has always enjoyed greater artistic and public success than heaven" because the "hope" Paul associates with heaven will not accommodate itself to any "judicial, objective conception" based upon prevailing notions of distributive justice (94). In other words, Paul's declaration of the hope of heaven radically redefines the colloquial expression, "we get what's coming to us." We shall look further at such a redefinition when we come to Chapters 4 and 5. When read in context, even Badiou's one passing mention of "heaven" provides an indication of a resonance with points in the theology of heaven just discussed that becomes increasingly discernible throughout his book. Most obviously is this the case when he describes "the only real of any import" as a "happening" that is "incalculable" (65).

Badiou's description of the Apostle Paul's declaration of the Resurrection and the fidelity it entails as "genuinely stupefying" is applicable as well to his own exposé of this news as he finds it in the Pauline epistles (9). His talk of "the only real of any import" in light of Paul's message is indeed stupefying, both as astonishing and nonsensical, when viewed from either its discordance with prevailing secular and religious frames of reference (of which he is quite aware), or from its unquestionable resonance with influential claims (of which he appears unaware) from theology's "narrow corner" that he so adamantly forswears. This slender volume bristles with conceptual realignments.

It comes from an unlikely quarter. A mathematician by training, as well as the author of novels and plays along with his numerous philosophical works, Badiou from the time of the student uprisings in Paris in 1968 has been associated with those identified politically as French Maoists. If we need to assign him to a category, he is a post (not pre!) -postmodernist of the Marxist–Leninist political left who goes against, by going beyond and not ignoring, influential trends in the current intellectual ethos with its analytical, hermeneutical, and, most importantly, postmodernist preoccupations with "difference" in opposition to so-called totalizing discourses and master narratives. But categorization, even as wordy as this, does not as such get to the truth, which is precisely Badiou's most impressive contention.

His argument, which I have written about in more detail elsewhere and repeat here for illustration only in its crux,[46] is that the "truth" exemplified in Paul's declaration of Christ's resurrection inheres in its nonconformity with any previous states of affairs, "prior markings" or "pre-constituted historical aggregates," as Badiou puts it (23, 6). This nonconformist "singularity," Badiou emphasizes, is what "universally" distinguishes real breakthroughs of "truth," whenever and wherever they occur, from simply the "knowledge" acquired through the assimilation of data that we process according to established formats. When Paul, who encountered the crucified Christ only in the power of his resurrection, writes that "Jews demand signs and Greeks desire wisdom, but we proclaim Christ crucified, a stumbling block (*skandalon*) to Jews and foolishness (*mōrian*) to Gentiles" (1 Cor. 1.22-23), he is declaring such a breakthrough of the two most established formats of subjective stances toward the world prevalent in his day. In Badiou's reading, Paul is not referring to Jews and Greek Gentiles as two ethnic groups, but as two distinguishable ways of regarding what counts as reality, ways that he labels "subjective dispositions" and "regimes of discourse" (41).

To become a subject convicted by such a declaration of the Resurrection — in Paul's language, to become an "apostle" — is to exhibit the fidelity of a "subjective disposition" or "regime of discourse" that ruptures all pre-existing classifications of what really counts in material circumstances and is "out of place" in a manner that Badiou eloquently describes as a "nomadism" of grace (78).

The political implication for Badiou is clear. His theory of the militant subject standing against the *status quo* sees the enabling of this militancy arising from situations when what has counted for nothing in our procedures breaches what figures to be accounted for. These are the real and universal breakthrough moments of "truth." They are precisely the happenings Paul declares of Christ's resurrection when he writes of "things that are not" reducing to nothing "things that are" (1 Cor. 1.28). What is "universal" in all the differences and multiple inconsistencies of our material situations is truth's irruption in conviction always as noncompliant event. For Badiou such irruptions of resurrection grace do not need recourse to a gracious "All-Powerful" but simply happen to us all at the contingent sites of our material circumstances (66). In *Saint Paul* Badiou makes his case with a Pauline vocabulary. In other works he develops the same points more abstractly in a complex ontology that draws upon mathematical accounts of infinity to reason that multiples in any situation (and Badiou specifically addresses situations of love, art, science, and politics) can be shown not to be constricted to a prefigured series of enumeration already followable in place, but to occur in settings in which what is out of order and out of place, in the sense of infinitely unaccountable and counting for nothing, provides the indispensable condition for new orderings and the emergence of the unprecedented.

Readers more familiar with theological discussions of the Gospel news of a *basileia* from heaven at hand than with the secular rhetorics of continental philosophy in which Badiou engages will be quick to spot in *Saint Paul* some intriguing likenesses of expression. One can excerpt much that reads like a transcription of theological discussions of eschatology and apocalyptic that greeted Moltmann's proposals regarding the future as *adventus* in the late sixties. Christ is said to be "a coming [*une venue*]" (48) that "happens to us universally" (60) whose resurrection is "the opening of an epoch" that "transforms all relations" (45) and is the occasioning of "radical novelty" (53).

Dissonances, to be sure, are to be noted as well, with respect to the existentialist construals of myth by Bultmann and Tillich, the absence of narrative, as in Barth's saga, and the lack of a language of promise with its commitments, as articulated by Moltmann. It is, of course, a truncated gospel that, in assertedly rendering the agency of grace as God-less, finally can speak of what is realistically "at hand" only in terms of what is in our hands: ". . . the Good News comes down to this: we *can* vanquish death" (45).

Even so, in the fabulousness (*point fabuleux*) (4) that Badiou delineates in Paul's news of the Resurrection there is a resonance with Barth's depiction of an envisagement of reality involving "divinatory imagination." And by arguing that the sheer gift of eventuating grace in Christ's resurrected coming constitutes a "new creature" of collaborative militancy, a subject disposed to a faithful "working together," not under a law of legitimacy, but according to an illegitimate grace (63–64), one may see a link as well with Barth's claims of the active engagement in current affairs that he refers to as "faithful disbelief." Despite the obvious differences in terminology and frames of reference, much of Badiou's "secular" talk of the "real" when taken in context does not sound as foreign as might be supposed to the deliteralized parabolic significance of "the real world" that we find in Barth's redefined demythologization.

2. *"The Significance of Virtual Reality"*

A second example of reality talk is the secular reappropriation today of the old theological language of *virtus* in the "virtual reality" discourse that accompanied the twentieth-century rise of the computer age and the Internet. We commonly say that something is "virtually" so when to all intents and purposes it is so in effect, even if not in established or establishable fact. Virtuality bridges a linguistic gap between what we call "net effect" and what we call "fact." Bultmann's urging of theologians "to make clear with what concept of reality, of being and events, we really operate in theology, and how this relates to the concepts in which . . . people think and speak of reality . . . in [their] everyday lives," leads us to this use of the term "virtual." How, we may ask, does it relate to the theological claim that the parabolic and apocalyptic significance of the Gospel news of heaven has to do with a "reality" that is not empirically verifiable, objectively cosmological, subjectively anthropological, or merely our own make-believe or social construct? The lingo of "virtual reality" at the start of the new millennium's much-heralded cybernetic age offers an especially pertinent example for comparison because it is a secular derivative of a theological expression that has been applied, no less, to heavenly reality in the past.[47]

Benjamin Woolley's book *Virtual Worlds* speaks to this point.[48] Woolley writes:

"Virtual" has a respectable pedigree as a technical term, going right back to the origins of modern science. It was used in optics at the beginning of the eighteenth century to describe the refracted or reflected image of an object. By the beginning of the nineteenth century, physicists were writing of a particle's "virtual velocity" and "virtual movement". The word is still used in physics to describe the exotic behavior of subatomic particles that appear so fleetingly they cannot be detected. It has come a long way from its original use as the adjectival form of "virtue" in the days when virtue itself meant to have the power of God.[49]

Woolley concludes, "The significance of virtual reality — and it is one hard to overstate . . . — is that it directly confronts the question: what is reality?"[50] With this significance a conversation, at least, with a theology of the Gospel's proclamation of a heavenly coming at hand is joined.

Here the reformer John Calvin (1509–1564) must be brought into our conversation, for it is Calvin most notably who, drawing upon earlier traditions,[51] employs the word *virtus* in accounting for a true coming of heaven. In sacramental debates over the presence of Christ in the communion of the Lord's Supper, Calvin argued as follows.[52]

Christian faith professes to find its life in the bodily reality of Jesus Christ. At the same time, the Gospel which the church proclaims locates that life as now risen and ascended in heaven. How then is this life in heaven, to use the church's manner of speaking, to be understood as today present here on earth? We seem at the least to have either a nonsense problem or a space problem — at any rate, nothing that really matters as far as the bodily flesh and blood reality of this present time is concerned. But to those who find in the confession of the presence of this heavenly life a matter of life and death importance, one way to proceed is to recognize what faith does *not* believe to be trustworthy. Such faith does not believe that the presence of heaven's life on earth is the product of any effect from earth. Nor is this presence real to us as something that can be calibrated or detected by any means of earthly measurement at our disposal. On the other hand, such faith refuses equally to believe that this presence of heaven's life is only a product of our imaginations. Still further, there is the refusal of faith to believe that this language of heaven is merely a sign of something else, or of somewhere else, a way of pointing to a day now past, or to a future day not present now, evoking only memories of other times and other places.

These deliberations come in his discussion of how most faithfully to attest to the real presence, or in his words, the true presence, of Jesus Christ in the communion of the Lord's Supper. Calvin insisted on maintaining the Gospel frame of reference of our life in the crucified Christ now ascended into heaven. He resisted attempts that tended, in his view, either to circumscribe or to generalize as some amorphous indeterminacy this heavenly locus in speaking of the real presence of Christ in the sacrament.[53] But he equally resisted tendencies to think of the Lord's Supper as a mere memorial, without the true heavenly presence of Christ. No, he argues, this feeding which, in his words, is immeasurable by "our measure," and "towers above all our senses,"[54] and is not just a matter of our "imagination," or a mere "appearance," or a bare "notion," is a participation in the "substance" of this heavenly life[55] that, as he puts it, penetrates into our very "bones and marrow."[56]

As Calvin characterizes this presence, it is a life that comes to us "vested in Christ's promises"[57] that manifests the power of Christ's Holy Spirit to fulfill these promises. The Latin word Calvin uses in writing of this reality of promised presence is the word *virtus*, the word meaning "the power to make effective." Because of his accounting of the present reality of the heavenly life of Christ coming to us by the Holy Spirit as the reality of *virtus*, Calvin's position has come to be known in some textbooks of doctrine as "virtualism."[58]

How parabolic John Calvin would find cyber-talk, and how indebted to Calvin the computer age is capable of recognizing itself to be, I will not venture to say.[59] But by eavesdropping we may hear something that, at least, bestirs us today in our narrow dogmatic slumbers.

If the news of the Gospel is that which overarches and is inclusive of all God's creation is the grace of heaven now "at hand" at ground level, such a reality cannot be said to be under our control, and certainly not under the control of our religion or computers, not in any respect "in hand." Here cyber-talk has yet to learn from Calvin. This "real world" is not the cybernetic virtuality of a simulated environment subject to our human programming. But, equally, is this the case with our theologies when, in Paul's words, "peddling" (or "promoting," καπηλεύοντες) as God's word (2 Cor. 2.17) their own social constructions of reality. In this hearing of the Gospel the heavenly life coming to us is not our construct. It is no artificial intelligence subject to our artifice or design. Parables of God's grace are God's doing and occur throughout every nation, but only and always *under* heaven.

To recapitulate our thought experiment from Chapter 1 up to this point, we observed in the beginning how, in contrast to the familiar associations that usually come to mind when we hear the word "heaven," some significantly additional promptings may be heard in listening again to the biblical testimonies that speak of heaven. Heaven indeed does not fit into our prevailing frames of reference for talking about the world, whether cosmological, anthropological, or historical. But that may be taken to mean, not that heaven lacks reality, but that reality may be more than our prevailing frames of reference. The intimation arising today from both a biblical call to "test the spirits" as well as from a postmodern permission, so to speak, to listen again to such scriptural testimony without the usual modernist earplugs is that not all actuality is factuality. Nor is this "real" as simply make-believe. What overarches this earth, if the *basileia* of heaven at hand is taken for real, is a dominion where the right of love and freedom is unimpeded, a dominion focused not upon the all blue yonder of the sky, but directed toward countering every impediment to the right of love and freedom with its justice now on this earth. The promptings of this hearing suggest that what is being referred to in the biblical testimony of the coming of heaven at hand is not so much the end of the "the real world" as its beginning, not the source of indifference and irresponsibility toward the present, but the source of an ability-to-respond to what the present calls for beyond all human powers of control that are, so to speak, "in hand."

All who in their glad hallelujahs of Resurrection give witness to the power of a strange, new world not yet observable as a conclusive fact within the frame of reference provided by the "form of this world [that] is passing away" (1 Cor. 7.31), will not be unfamiliar with the original significance of Calvin's use of the word "virtual," or fail to recognize its contrast with the "virtual reality" discourse of today. As Woolley observed, "It has come a long way from its original use as the adjectival form of 'virtue' in the days when virtue itself meant to have the power of God."

In this strange interruption of *virtus* as a heavenly power Calvin recognized a decisive contrast with Aristotle's treatment of virtue as an anthropological characteristic. This leads us next to question the difference this "real world" of heaven makes today for ethics.

Chapter 4

THE ETHICS OF HEAVEN

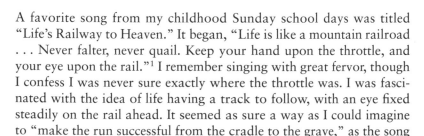

A favorite song from my childhood Sunday school days was titled "Life's Railway to Heaven." It began, "Life is like a mountain railroad . . . Never falter, never quail. Keep your hand upon the throttle, and your eye upon the rail."[1] I remember singing with great fervor, though I confess I was never sure exactly where the throttle was. I was fascinated with the idea of life having a track to follow, with an eye fixed steadily on the rail ahead. It seemed as sure a way as I could imagine to "make the run successful from the cradle to the grave," as the song so graphically put it.

The idea of life keeping on a track that is firmly in place and directed ever upward is reflected in much of our more sophisticated talk about a universal moral law and moral order. And it is often reflected as well in the social commentary wherever there are those who speak indignantly about how the plain and clear distinction between right and wrong, good and bad, truth and falsehood becomes increasingly ignored at the present time in a culture that is morally derailed with the ten commandments, as the quip goes, having been reduced to the ten suggestions.

The previous chapter began by noting the New Testament scholar J. Louis Martyn's observation that in sharp contrast to the assumption that a good religious foundation provides a ladder of ascent by which its adherents can move out of the wrong into blessedness — a track, in other words, climbing ever onward and upward to make the run successful from the cradle to the grave — the Apostle Paul's news to the Galatians turns this whole scenario on its head. Rather, the Gospel tells of a movement from the opposite direction, a liberating invasion of the cosmos by God's sending of the Son and the Spirit of the Son from outside it (Gal. 1.4). This liberating invasion of the cosmos that cannot be tracked prior to its coming Martyn characterizes as "apocalyptic." Thus it comes as no surprise in turning to Paul's message to the Galatians regarding behavioral matters to find Martyn writing that: ". . . The picture Paul presents in Gal. 5.13-24 is so thoroughly permeated by apocalyptic motifs as to be seriously domesticated when it is pressed into the categories usually associated with morals and ethics. For Paul's picture, rather than being basically hortatory, is in the first instance a description of daily life in the real world, made what it is by the advent of Christ and his Spirit."[2]

While the proposed thought experiment of these pages focuses more broadly on a dogmatic appraisal of how the Gospel testimony regarding heaven may be said to make a difference today, this textual commentary by Martyn aptly provides a segue into the more general question of what the foregoing discussion of the Gospel news of heaven has to do with ethics.

The study of ethics as reflection on the good life and on doing good comprises a rich and complex history of moral reasoning in Western philosophy dating back to the time of Socrates.[3] Whether viewed as theistic or not, the major ethical positions in this history have primarily concentrated anthropologically upon theories of human agency. For Aristotle, the aim or *telos* of ethics is the good of the individual within the social relationships that make for the wellbeing of a society (*polis*) based upon what its citizens do as virtuous acts. The virtue Aristotle characterizes is a human disposition, "up to us and voluntary."[4] In contrast, the Gospel news of heaven, so we have seen Calvin argue, tells of another *virtus*, a disposing by God's forthcoming that is not up to us and our volition.[5] Posing the question of ethics as the relation of a heavenly doing, or the *virtus* of a heavenly *politeia*, with our doing on earth, as participation in accord with this *politeia* and *basileia* at hand, sets the parameters and focus for this chapter. If — to recap previous points — hearing the Gospel news of heaven involves us in a state of affairs or "real world" of parabolic and apocalyptic significance, this includes both an *envisagement* of what is taking place at the present time and an *engagement* in what is happening. Being faced with the proximity of an incalculable inbreaking that cannot be approximated, a refusal to trust what is standing in the way of this happening is called forth, a posture of faithful disbelief. The question becomes, what direction for "daily life in the real world," as Martyn puts it, do these parameters regarding heaven offer?

The Direction of Heaven

This question of heaven's direction is primary. To those who pray, "Thy kingdom come, thy will be done on earth as it is in heaven," the issue of the relation of what is done in heaven and what is done on earth cannot be ignored. The sequence of petitions in the Lord's Prayer bears noticing, not as a proof text but as an indicator of a precedence that we find elsewhere throughout the Gospel. Prayer to "Our Father in heaven" for the *basileia's* coming precedes mention of the will of heaven being done on earth. The coming, that is to say, sets the context for what is to be done. The direction is from there to here, not, as life's railway would have it, from here to there. Or, more exactly, the there is proclaimed as here, by such expressions as "in our midst," "coming to pass," "in due season," and "in the fullness of time," but not, as we have observed, according to the fig tree's regular seasons, or in a manner compliant with "the course (*aiōn*) of this world's" stipulations (Eph. 2.2). From a number of New Testament instances where this heavenly direction is highlighted, I select three examples for illustration that specifically address the "doing" that is said to be called forth in a faithful hearing of the Gospel.

1. *Observing the Sabbath*

Conflicting directions informing moral judgments concerning the good and doing good confront us in hearing the news of Jesus' healing the man with the withered hand on the Sabbath. Parallel accounts appear in Matthew 12.9-14, Mark 3.1-6, and Luke 6.6-11, whose version goes as follows:

> 6. On another Sabbath he entered the synagogue and taught, and there was a man there whose right hand was withered. 7. The scribes and the Pharisees watched him to see whether he would cure on the Sabbath, so that they might find an accusation against him. 8. Even though he knew what they were thinking, he said to the man who had the withered hand, "Come and stand here." He got up and stood there. 9. Then Jesus said to them, "I ask you, is it lawful to do good or to do harm on the Sabbath, to save life or to destroy it?" 10. After looking around at all of them, he said to him, "Stretch out your hand." He did so, and his hand was restored. 11. But they were filled with fury and discussed with one another what they might do to Jesus.

Both Jesus and his accusers are depicted as looking at the same situation but seeing it very differently. By the accusers' frame of reference, what was really happening was a breaking of the law. As they saw the situation, the question it posed was plain: should someone break the law or not? It is important not to trivialize and underestimate the import of the story by simplistically casting in a negative stereotype the accusers' moral position. Theirs was the question of moral duty, and as such not to be disparaged. The issue was not about any law; this was the law of God, God's own commandment to honor the Sabbath and do no work on it.

And Jesus was not simply any violator. According to the Gospel accounts he was called "Teacher" by his followers, and we hear that at times the crowds surrounding him were large. Furthermore, the accusers, being scribes and Pharisees, could be understood to have a special responsibility for trying to uphold the law and seeing that as God's will it was observed. If you allow so public a figure in the position of a teacher to break the law, how could the crowds be expected to obey it? We know the arguments.

By Jesus' response to the accusers, however, a different frame of reference is introduced: "I ask you, is it lawful to do good or to harm on the Sabbath, to save life or to destroy it?" That obviously is not the question that the accusers see the situation posing. In their terms, such a question must be said to constitute an infuriating evasion. It simply misses the point. Yet this question of Jesus, as in other incidents depicted in the Gospels, redirects the point about observance by asking the accusers, in effect, whether, having eyes to see and ears to hear, they actually are observing what is really taking place. Observance is indeed what is at stake, but observance of a very different kind. A fulfillment of the Sabbath is taking place in this healing. Are they observing that happening? "But they were filled with fury," the account concludes, by observing a doing taking place on the Sabbath, in noncompliance with the stipulations for Sabbath observance that they hold to be in place. Hence we are told that they "discussed with one another what they might do to Jesus" (Lk. 6.11).

Contested directions governing moral judgment, whether tending toward keeping to tracks of legitimation in place, or tending toward asking whether harm or good is being done in the situation currently taking place, are represented throughout the history of moral theology and ethics. In this incident of Luke's depiction, the moral train is clearly off track from the accusers' perspective, which leads to the second example from hearing the Gospel testimonies, one that explicitly deals with situational discernment.

2. Discerning What is Best

In everyday speech we commonly describe how we see a situation as "sizing it up." Our vernacular exposes the dilemma that hearing the Gospel news of an immeasurable heaven presents for any attempt to draw up its practical consequences. How does such "sizing" follow from what we hear? If it finally results only in a moral maxim, such as "everyone should do good and not do harm," then what Dickinson called "Much Gesture, from the Pulpit —" is reduced indeed to merely the "hortatory" status that Martyn finds so opposed to the news of "life in the real world" that Paul vigorously declares to the Galatians.

A New Testament word for discerning what is happening at the present time and also for determining what to do about it is *dokimazein* (δοκιμάζειν). It is this same word that is used in 1 John 4.1 for "testing" the spirits to see whether they are from God or instead represent the claims of false prophets abroad in the world (1 Jn 4.1). Within the Gospel contexts of its usage this word encompasses what we have called both an *envisagement* and also an *engagement* with respect to what is currently taking place. An emphasis upon discernment as envisagement appears in Jesus' reported rebuke of the crowds who are more concerned, we are told, with the way the wind is blowing than in recognizing what is really going on in their midst. As we hear, Jesus said to the crowds, "When you see a cloud rising in the west, you immediately say, 'It is going to rain'; and so it happens. And when you see the south wind blowing you say, 'There will be scorching heat'; and it happens. You hypocrites! You know how to interpret (*dokimazein*) the appearance of the earth and sky, but why do you not know how to interpret (*dokimazein*) the present time?" (Lk. 12.54-56). An emphasis upon discernment as engagement occurs in Paul's words of assurance to the Philippians of his prayer for them, "that your love may overflow more and more with knowledge and full insight to help you to determine (*dokimazein*) what is best so that in the day of Christ you may be pure and blameless . . ." (Phil.1.9-10).

Excerpted in mid-sentence and abstracted from its context, this reference to "determining" what love seeks as "best" taken by itself easily reduces to just another moral maxim, again hortatory in nature, an admonition that what is decisive and determinative in any situation at hand is *our* application of love as a "normative ideal" in a manner fitting for that situation. In the sixties such a widely debated "situation ethics" was most popularly advocated by Joseph Fletcher as a "strategy of love" that provided an ethical alternative to both a legalism governed by rules and principles, on the one hand, and an antinomianism opposed to all maxims and moral guidelines, on the other.[6] While in a postscript

Fletcher did allow that "before we ask the ethical question, 'What shall I do?' comes the *pre*ethical question, 'What has God done?,'" nothing figures as God's doing in the situation, as Fletcher describes it, other than the command to love God and neighbor — certainly nothing figures that has to do with news of heaven.[7]

In retrospect, it is remarkable to see this lacuna in most discussions at the time of a situational ethics. A telling quote from Fletcher in defining the "strategy of love" implies an equation of appeals to heaven with moral legalism. "This strategy denies that there are . . . any unwritten immutable laws of heaven, agreeing with Bultmann that all such notions are idolatrous and a demonic pretension."[8] Yet critics at the time who caricatured situational ethics as "sloppy *agápe*" (αγάπη, "love") for its lack of rules and principles were equally silent with respect to how the Gospel news of a forthcoming from heaven at hand made any difference to their ethical principles.

The context of Paul's message here to the Philippians challenges both the direction of a situational ethics as well as that of an ethics directed by moral principles, for neither of these, despite their opposition, accords with Paul's frame of reference that "our *politeia* (*citizenship* or *commonwealth*) is in heaven, and it is from there that we are expecting a Savior, the Lord Jesus Christ, [who] will transform our humble bodies that they may be conformed to his glorious body, by the power that also enables him to make all things subject to himself" (Phil. 3.20-21). When this contextual framework is dismissed as dispensable mythic husk, Paul's full sentence loses its heavenly referent, where we hear, "And this is my prayer, that your love may overflow more and more with knowledge and full insight to help you to determine (*dokimazein*) what is best, *so that in the day of Christ you may be pure and blameless, having produced the harvest of righteousness that comes through Jesus Christ for the glory and praise of God*" (Phil. 1.9-11). This is a "day," Paul writes to the Romans, that is "at hand" (13.12). This is a "Lord," so he writes to the Philippians, who is "at hand" (Phi. 4.5). It is precisely this *at-handedness* that sets the direction for love's determining in the present situation what is best, an *at-handedness* equally disregarded by interpreters who stress love as only a norm and ideal to be applied situationally, as well as by their opposing advocates of a more rule-driven ethics.

This contextual usage of *dokimazein*, as both *interpreting* the present time and *determining* what love seeks as best, provides a second illustration of how the hearing of the Gospel news of heaven affects the direction of ethical discernment as to the doing "on earth."

3. The "Coming" and "Doing" in Matthew 25.31-46

A third example is especially intriguing in the questions it prompts about the relation of a heavenly coming to ethics as our earthly doing. With graphic specificity, Jesus' parable in Matthew 25.31-46 regarding what is done on earth with respect to "the least" — the hungry, the thirsty, the stranger, the naked, the sick, and the imprisoned — announces that the coming judgment to all nations is this: "Just as you did it [or did not do it] to one of the least of these who are my family, you did it [or did not do it] to me" (Mt. 25.40, 45).

Extracted from its context, this statement taken alone also quickly reduces to a hortatory moralism: one ought always to do good to those in need, to the least among us. With such an admonition few would disagree, and it hardly comes as news to anyone old enough to hear it. Being told that we ought to care about the less fortunate is a message familiar to hearers of sermons on this passage, even those sermons accompanied by "Much Gesture, from the Pulpit —." For the purposes of morality and ethics, it would thus appear that any additional reference to a coming from heaven is ethically extraneous, irrelevant, and indeed may even divert us from doing what we should.

Yet, taken in its context, this pericope in the Gospel of Matthew occurs in a sequence of parables expressly referring to the *basileia* of heaven, and in this particular parable the apocalyptic setting for its moral judgment is introduced by the following words of Jesus: "When the Son of Man comes in his glory, and all the angels with him, then he will sit on the throne of his glory. All the nations will be gathered before him . . ." (Mt. 25.31-32). Is our hearing of a coming judgment in these introductory words of Jesus extraneous to the real point, which is a more obvious and familiar moral lesson about how hearers of the parable should treat the least? And if not, what difference for ethics does the added hearing of a heavenly coming make in this case?

One possible answer is that a content is given to the crucial phrase of the Lord's Prayer "as it is in heaven." What is currently being done and not done on earth with regard to the least is what we hear is identifiable and not identifiable with what is being done in heaven. If this is the message, then prayer that our doing on earth is "as it is in heaven" is not simply the mantra of an empty cipher without content or direction. There is an unambiguous concreteness about what is being done on earth as in heaven, and how that heavenly doing is to be judged as currently taking place. Heavenly doing is a doing "unto the least." Such a hearing of how heaven's coming is currently taking place dislocates moral judgment from its familiarity with claims as to what is normative and repositions it instead to a surprised questioning about what is formative in the situation at hand — "Lord, when did we see you . . .?" Absent heaven's inbreaking the least retains a relegated status in moral theory as the necessary prerequisite for the virtuous expressions of charity by the more fortunate. The blessedness of the poor is mistaken for a longsuffering by which they track their way to heaven (Mt. 5.3). Hearing news of the *at-handedness* of heaven's forthcoming, as *politeia*, *basileia*, and new creation, in relation to the least, or what Paul calls "the sufferings of this present time" (Rom. 8.18), does not deify oppression or sacralize suffering as a permanent state in place. It points instead to how heaven as a contravention is now making its way. It also shows by this taking place where the power for setting at liberty the oppressed is coming from (Lk. 4.18).

What we hear in these three examples of scriptural testimony is not the discourse of ontological abstraction about irruptions of exceptionality or incalculable inbreaking, but news of such occurrence expressed in a more graphic register of deeds and of judgment in their practical concreteness. In each instance, though distinctly specified, we hear of what comes upon the scene as that which happens to disclose what is being done on the scene. A real world of difference emerges between a normative moralism, whether primarily situational or rule-driven, that is expressed through exhortation about what *ought* to happen, and the word that a heavenly state of affairs at hand actually *is* happening. If we take the label of "ethics" to denote not merely a hortatory moralism, but more comprehensively a characterization of doing, then "a description of daily life in the real world," in Martyn's words, requires that questions arising from hearing of a doing that is said to be "as in heaven" be addressed.

Reversing Directions: Weiss's Problematic

The problematic posed in 1892 by Johannes Weiss's monograph *Jesus' Proclamation of the Kingdom of God* set the table, as we have seen, for a trajectory of theological responses that comprises one of the twentieth century's most important legacies. At its crux is the issue of the Kantian reversal of Gospel apocalyptic, which redirected the cosmic hearing of the news of the kingdom of God at hand into the moral components of a universal ethical state more comparable to a "seed which is self-developing and in due time self-fertilizing."[9] In the worldview articulated by Kant, the Gospel talk of heaven denotes a transcendence from which the exercise of moral judgment must keep "a respectful distance" lest we "allow ourselves to fall into the indolence of awaiting from above, in passive leisure, what we should seek within."[10]

It was Weiss who created a stir in the theology of an era largely influenced by Kant's reversal by arguing that "the modern Protestant world-view's" attempts to reinterpret the kingdom as an "ethical commonwealth" to be realized by the moral doing of human subjects could not be said to be the *basileia* of the Gospel proclamation. At the same time, notwithstanding, he also conceded that "the modern Protestant world-view" could not reasonably accommodate the Gospel news of "a Kingdom of God which is to come down from heaven to earth to abolish this world."[11] Modernity does not share the "eschatological attitude, namely, that τό σχῆμα τοῦ κόσμου τούτου παράγει" ["the form of this world is passing away," or "the current cosmic scheme is passing away."][12] Most tellingly, while insisting upon the acknowledgement that the "ethical side," as he expressed it, of the "modern Protestant world-view's" reconception of the *basileia* was "thoroughly unbiblical . . . inasmuch as the notion of an 'actualization of the Rule of God' by human ethical activity is completely contrary to the transcendentalism of Jesus' idea," Weiss nevertheless concluded that such a modern reconception of the kingdom of God was the only sensible idea of the term for today. "Only the admission must be demanded that we use it in a different sense from Jesus."[13]

This reversal of direction in envisaging the kingdom — from a *basileia* coming from heaven and now actually at hand that is formative of a doing on earth that is the will of heaven to, by contrast, a *basileia* as an end or outcome that is normative of the moral doing required to achieve its actualization as "an ethical commonwealth" — had two major results. (1) It effectively sidetracked the Gospel references to heaven from serious theological consideration as being news of "real-world" consequence, and (2) it introduced what Weiss called a "thoroughly unbiblical" understanding of ethics.

On the first point, Weiss himself shows an inconsistency regarding the significance of hearing that the kingdom of God is a kingdom from heaven. He writes, as a textual historian, that since the term "kingdom of heaven" is distinctive only to the Gospel of Matthew he does not regard "the characteristics which might perhaps be derived from the phrase βασιλεία τῶν οὐρανῶν (*basileia of heaven*) to be features of the original idea."[14] Yet when it comes to saying what it is that dogmatically distinguishes the original Gospel teaching regarding the kingdom from that of its modern interpreters, it is precisely the reference to heaven, he contends, that makes the difference in that "the modern Protestant world-view" no longer awaits a *basileia* coming from heaven to earth. Thus, in concurring with the prevailing consensus that the original Gospel expectation must have been mistaken, and in proposing that modern theology has no sensible alternative but to reject the idea of a coming from heaven and think instead of the kingdom in another sense as a developing "religious and ethical fellowship," Weiss's monograph provides a multidimensional backdrop for recognizing how the Gospel news of heaven registers in subsequent theological accounts of "daily life in the real world" as a characterization of earthly doing.

In the trajectory of twentieth-century responses considered in Chapter 2 regarding ways of hearing the Gospel news of heaven, we noted first of all an agreement among the proponents of myth, symbol, saga, and promise in rejecting a univocal literalism. Their concurrence in opposing a literalistic hearing of heaven is based, not simply upon the fact that such an interpretation is no longer credible in the critical reasoning of "the modern Protestant world-view," but that the content of the original Gospel news itself is shown to require it. There is further agreement in affirming with Weiss the eschatological significance of the Gospel proclamation, though each of the four ways in their distinctive terms of existential myth and symbol, saga, and promise attributes to this proclaimed Word a more dynamic sense than does Weiss of its efficacy as a present event or happening.

Yet the difference in the role heaven plays in these four responses is no less significant. For Bultmann, where the Gospel references to heaven tend to be viewed least positively, the eschatological sense of the *basileia* as Word-event or happening is translated into existential terms which effectively sideline heaven talk to associations with the sky as pre-scientific cosmological myth of an outdated three-level worldview requiring demythologization. For Tillich the symbolic retrieval of biblical references to heaven plays a role within his existential ontology that carries more of the overtones of an association of heaven with a qualitative state of bliss; heaven is credited as a symbol for a more stable state of blessedness, and as such is only briefly mentioned. "'God is in heaven'; this means that his life is qualitatively different from creaturely existence. But it does not mean that he 'lives in' or 'descends from' a special place."[15]

Karl Barth, as we have noted, stands out among his non-literalist colleagues in 1940 in demurring from the critical consensus of the time that alleged the Gospel's mistaken expectations and writing that "the categorical assertion that this expectation of something at hand 'was not fulfilled' is to obvious to be convincing." For Barth, we have seen, myth does not trump saga, nor, echoing Franz Overbeck, can historicist categories as generally conceived presume to accommodate a more primal history-making Gospel testimony. By explicitly referring to the dogmatic significance of the kingdom of God as "of heaven," and with such assertions regarding the kingdom as, "And in coming to us, it brings heaven with it," Barth provides a notable exception to the general disassociation of the news of heaven from that of the kingdom of God that occurs in modern theology following Weiss.

With respect to the particular subject of ethics, however, it must be pointed out that Barth remained wary of speaking of the doing of heaven even when, as in his case, that "doing," contrary to Kant's reversal, was acknowledged to come, not from ourselves, but from heaven. As early as 1921, in the second edition of his commentary on Romans, completed while he was still a village pastor, he had written:[16]

> All human doing or not-doing is simply an occasion or opportunity of pointing to that which alone is worthy of being called "action,"namely, the action of God. In the sphere of ethics this rule is adamant . . . Whenever men claim to be able to see the Kingdom of God as a growing organism, or — to describe it more suitably — as a growing building, what they see is not the Kingdom of God, but the Tower of Babel . . . Pure ethics require — and here we are in complete agreement with Kant — that there should be no mixing of heaven and earth in the sphere of morals.

Though he would later go on to refine and greatly expand upon his earlier views, and not ride simply one eschatological "hobby horse," as he put it,[17] this early statement from his Romans commentary remains consistent with the substantial treatment given to ethics in his later lectures and in lengthy parts of his multi-volume *Church Dogmatics*.[18] Our doing on earth cannot claim the power of heaven as if we could by our moral effort "take it by force" (Mt. 11.12). But the power of heaven can and does claim our moral effort for its parabolic witnesses as pointers to the action of God, a threefold claiming that Barth develops in great detail with respect to God's acts in Jesus Christ of creating, reconciling, and redeeming.

Still, a generation later, in 1964, it is Jürgen Moltman's *Theology of Hope* that boldly reignites the problematic posed by Weiss, Schweitzer, and Overbeck, with the claim that it is "precisely the transcendentalist view of eschatology that prevented the breakthrough of eschatological dimensions in dogmatics" by not attending sufficiently to the performative history-making character of the Gospel news as promise.[19] Challenged in turn to account for the "real-world" role of human responsibility in the face of such a promised future as *adventus*, Moltmann's writings over the next thirty years develop a series of responses, culminating in his most comprehensive treatment in 1996, *The Coming of God: Christian Eschatology.*[20]

By the end of the twentieth century the Gospel references to heaven that had stirred up such a controversy with Weiss a hundred years earlier had ceased to figure as explicitly in the debates over the dogmatic significance of eschatology, whether viewed as transcendentalist or not. More exactly, this was the case within the non-literalistic theological renderings of these references that had followed in the wake of Weiss. Apart from the more conventional associations of heaven with only the sky, the hereafter, or a qualitative state of bliss, theological questions remained as to what was really newsworthy as far as an ethics of "daily life in the real world" was concerned in further hearing of heaven as the directional course of God's forthcoming, proclaimed to be now at hand as God's own creation, *politeia* or community, and *basileia* or dominion.

On the second point, Weiss's claim that the Kantian reversal introduces a "thoroughly unbiblical" understanding of ethics, the major issues at dispute and their import can best be distilled by turning to Dietrich Bonhoeffer.

Responsibility in the Real World: Bonhoeffer

At the time of his execution by the Nazis at Flossenbürg concentration camp on April 9, 1945 for his participation in the resistance against Hitler, Bonhoeffer, at age thirty-nine, had already given much theological attention to the question of what a thoroughly biblical ethics in today's world entails. His comments on ethics span nearly a twenty-year period, beginning in 1924 with his student days and later brief period of lecturing at Berlin University, and his experience as a visiting scholar at Union Seminary in New York in 1930–31, and again for several weeks in the summer of 1939 before abruptly returning to face the impending crisis of World War II in his native Germany. His early death prevented the completion of his major work on ethics, the partial drafts of which show his continuing revisions and emendations, and later interpreters have drawn differing conclusions from the collected papers that remain. We need not impose a definitive interpretation upon the variety of Bonhoeffer's statements regarding ethics in order to recognize the pertinence to our foregoing discussion of two of his most characteristic themes: *ethical responsibility derives from the reality of heaven that is currently facing us at ground level; and this reality is worldly in a way that is not restricted or generic to religion.* Both of these themes contrast with Kant's reversal, and both Bonhoeffer interprets Christologically.

In a series of lectures delivered in 1933 on the presence of Jesus Christ existing for us today as a community (*Gemeinde*), Bonhoeffer states: "His form (*Gestalt*), indeed his only form, is the community between the ascension and the second coming. The fact that he is in heaven on the right hand of God does not contradict this; on the contrary, it alone makes possible his presence in and as the community."[21] This statement is key in that, while Bonhoeffer seldom refers explicitly to heaven, it shows in this instance the decisive agency he attaches to it, an agency that alone is said to make possible, indeed actual, the very opposite of what Kant had called "the indolence of awaiting from above, in passive leisure, what we should seek within." The ethical ramifications of this claim Bonhoeffer develops throughout his writings. This may be seen from what he has to say about the nature of ethics with respect to what may be called Bonhoeffer's three R's: religion, reality, and responsibility. Of these three R's it is in Bonhoeffer's view the second, "reality," that defines in a thoroughly biblical ethics the other two.

"The reason for this," he writes, "is that *reality [die Wirklichkeit]* is first and last not something impersonal [Neutrum], but *the Real One [der Wirkliche]*, namely, the God who became human."[22] This entails that "the *orientation from above to below* . . . is an intrinsic and essential quality of the ethical, even though it is so highly offensive to the modern mind." We shall see that this expression of ethical "orientation" poses a tension in Bonhoeffer's overall thought that a recognition of heaven's at-handedness addresses.[23]

To follow his thinking we need first to look at the historical context. In summing up his experiences in the thirties, both in the United States and in his native Germany, we find Bonhoeffer writing: "The decisive task for today is the dialogue between Protestantism without Reformation and the churches of the Reformation."[24] As he discusses it, the expression "Protestantism without Reformation" may be seen to designate for Bonhoeffer the sort of "thoroughly unbiblical" view of Christian ethics that Weiss had associated with "the modern Protestant world-view."

Three sets of circumstances in the thirties provided the context for Bonhoeffer's judgment. The first was the background of his earliest scholarly writings. Though he was only twenty-four when he first arrived at Union, before coming Bonhoeffer had already completed a doctoral dissertation and prepared for publication a second book within a year.[25] In each of these early theological works he had opposed the divorce between theology and social analysis, and argued for the need to bring them together. As he put it, his aim was to draw sociology "into the service of dogmatics."[26] The second was his impression of how the almost exclusive emphasis of American Protestantism upon social issues and ethics as he initially experienced it at Union in 1930 exhibited a similar problem in reverse by essentially ignoring dogmatics in its sociology. At Union he encountered much social criticism and a commendable practicality about everyday matters but, to his dismay, hardly any attention given to the critical dogmatic question of what *God* is doing in society. Some "have turned their back on all genuine theology" in their study of "economic and political problems," he observes, while still calling their interpretation Christian Ethics.[27] Others hold to a "certain enlightened rationalism" in which, he writes, "the fact of an inner-theological criticism is completely unknown and misunderstood [and] the teaching of dogmatic principles is hopelessly confused."[28] Still another group appears to think that the philosophy of religion is more "scientific," and yet it speaks with a shocking "lack of seriousness" of God and the world. And finally, Bonhoeffer records his impression that those who most champion "practical theology" seem almost completely preoccupied with "modern methods" and seldom ask what the "content" of "the church's message" is.[29] The third circumstance was the ominous rise of the Nazi movement all the while back in his own country, with Hitler's coming to power, and the kind of threat it posed for the way the churches engaged in theology in facing up to their ethical responsibility.

The issue, as Bonhoeffer sees it, is freedom and a radically different kind of trust about where freedom comes from. In a "Protestantism without Reformation" the emphasis is mainly upon religion and ethics. "They remind us from over there," Bonhoeffer writes, "You overrate thought, theology, dogma; it is only one of many expressions of the church, and not the most important one at that. We reply: It is not a question of thought, but of the truth of the Word of God, by which we mean to live and die. It is a question of salvation. Granted, the unity of the church does not lie in human thought, but neither does it lie in human 'Life and Work'. It lies solely in the life and work of Jesus Christ, in which we participate through faith."[30] Despite their rightful intent to offer social and ethical criticism the representatives of a "Protestantism without Reformation" fail, in Bonhoeffer's words, "to understand the meaning of 'criticism' by the Word of God and all that signifies. Right to the last they do not understand that God's 'criticism' touches even religion, the Christianity of the churches and the sanctification of Christians, and that God has founded his church beyond religion and beyond ethics."[31]

By contrast, in the faith of the Reformation church the Word of God is recognized to have formative agency. The confidence of such faith lies not within the limits of religion or human achievement. "The freedom of the church," Bonhoeffer writes, "is not where it has possibilities, but only where the Gospel really and in its own power makes room for itself on earth, even and precisely when no such possibilities are offered to it."[32] God alone "makes and does the impossible" in calling the church from death to life "against and despite us and through us."[33]

Bonhoeffer found this faith in America, just a few blocks north of Union Seminary in the churches of Harlem. It was not the only place he found it, but it was the place, he tells us, that left an indelible mark upon him. In the preaching and spirituals of what was then called "the Negro church" he heard the proclamation of a Word of God that makes room for freedom on the earth precisely when and where no such possibilities are offered to it. He encountered a people witnessing to how the God of the Bible does the impossible and makes a way out of no way. ". . . Nowhere," he wrote, "is revival preaching still so vigorous and so widespread . . . Here the Gospel of Jesus Christ, the saviour of the sinner, is really preached and accepted with great welcome and visible emotion." Thus, "it is barely understandable that great negro singers can sing these songs before packed concert audiences of whites, to tumultuous applause, while at the same time these same men and women are still denied access to the white community through social discrimination." "Black and white hear the Word and receive the sacrament in separation." "The solution to [this] problem is one of the decisive future tasks of the white churches."[34]

What is God *doing in the present situation?* This for Bonhoeffer is the decisive question the Gospel poses for its followers wherever they are located. Addressing it is "the decisive task" of theology and its confessional responsibility, as he sees it, because everything else follows from the answer given. A "Protestantism without Reformation" that places its confidence in the power of religion to do good and save the world thereby gives a very different answer to the question of "what God is doing" from that of a "Reformation church" which knows itself called to life and service by the Savior of the world. ". . . At this point," Bonhoeffer writes, "there opens up an almost incalculable deep opposition between the churches of the Reformation and 'Protestantism without Reformation'."[35]

1. *Religion*

Religion is an inadequate frame of reference to account for this power and doing of God for three reasons. The first is scriptural, always a primary reason for Bonhoeffer. The Gospel accounts seldom mention religion, and in the few instances that they do it is usually contrasted with faith in Jesus Christ.[36] Thus Paul is said in *Acts* to have remarked to the Athenians about how extremely "religious" they were because they had even constructed an altar, along with all their other shrines, inscribed, "To an unknown god" (Acts 17.22). And the writer of the Letter of James, as well, differentiates religion as something we do from what he calls "the faith of our glorious Lord Jesus Christ" (James 1.26-27, 2.1).

A second reason for Bonhoeffer's judgment that "what God is doing" does not register as religion relates to the theological context in which he had been trained. Like all of us, Bonhoeffer did not hear and read the Gospels in a social vacuum. He had his teachers and was well versed in the most influential theological trends of his day. Like most well-educated theological students of his time Bonhoeffer had been taught to differentiate between "the real world" and the story of Jesus in the New Testament. Since much of that story could not be documented as historical fact, it had since the seventeenth century come to be treated by many in critical circles as a mythical world having to do, not with social affairs in any external sense of the world at large, but with inner experiences and matters of the heart. The world of Jesus was an internal world of religious experience and the soul. Kant in 1793 had written in *Religion within the Limits of Reason Alone*: "The Teacher of the Gospel revealed to his disciples the kingdom of God on earth only in its glorious, soul-elevating moral aspect, namely, in terms of the value of citizenship in a divine state, and to this end he informed them of what they had to do, not only to achieve it themselves but to unite with all others of the same mind and, so far as possible, with the entire human race."[37] Religious inwardness was the prevailing doctrine of Harnack, with whom Bonhoeffer had studied but on this point had respectfully disagreed.

Further back in history, of course, were the influential voices of the Reformation that shaped Bonhoeffer's thinking. John Calvin indeed granted that there was, what he called, a "seed of religion" in all human beings (*Inst.* I, 4), but he taught that this religious seed grows into superstition and idolatry unless God is "comprehended" (II, 6, 4) and joined together with us in "Christ alone" (II, 16, 3).[38] And it was Martin Luther's "theology of the cross" to which Bonhoeffer continually referred in stressing, in Luther's words, that only the "theologian of the cross" calls what is good and bad by their real names and recognizes that God is not to be found apart from sufferings and the cross.[39]

Today we may stumble at Reformation talk of "Christ alone" because of the way it has often been taken to mean "the Christian religion" alone, or "Christianity" alone, to the exclusion of all other religions and indigenous traditions. The results of such exclusiveness and bigotry can be seen in the bitter fruit of anti-Semitism and other forms of religious intolerance, cultural imperialism, and even warfare that have continued to plague human history. We can debate whether Bonhoeffer's Christocentrism in effect contributes to, or actually contradicts, such religious exclusiveness and intolerance. But the record is clear that for Bonhoeffer Jesus Christ is not to be equated with Christianity as a religion, or indeed with religion itself. Bonhoeffer himself came, though not without his own failings, to confront the Jewish persecution under the Nazis, and he longed to learn more from Ghandi and the spiritual traditions of India. The point is that for Bonhoeffer there is no place where God's Word is not Emmanuel, "God-With-Us," "becoming human" (*Menschwerdung*) in what Paul calls the "groaning in labor pains" of creation (Rom. 8.22).[40] This, as Bonhoeffer hears the Gospel, is who Jesus Christ is for us today, God's life socially embodied and formative communally in what is now taking place that spans all creation and is not confined religiously simply to those who may say, "Lord, Lord" (Mt. 7.21).

In this recognition Bonhoeffer also acknowledged his indebtedness to the newly emerging theological influence of Karl Barth. "Barth was the first theologian to begin the criticism of religion," Bonhoeffer writes, "and that remains his really great merit."[41] Although Bonhoeffer only knew the beginnings of Barth's dogmatic theology, differed with it in some aspects, and would not live to see its multi-volume completion, he had caught and embraced the crucial point. As Barth would later express it, "The statement that Jesus Christ is the one Word of God has really nothing whatever to do with the arbitrary exaltation and self-glorification of the Christian in relation to other human beings, of the Church in relation to other institutions, or of Christianity in relation to other conceptions."[42] On this crucial point Bonhoeffer's thinking early and late stood with Barth and against those who attempted to divide up the peoples of the world according to religions, or to interpret the world into which Jesus Christ comes as an internal religious world of the soul, a world restricted to Christianity.[43]

Bonhoeffer's third objection to interpreting "what God is doing" in religious terms had to do with his reading of the role that religion often plays in culture. In addition to scripture, and the theological influences of his day to which he was responding, there was also this cultural reason. As the Apostle Paul had noted in preaching to the Athenians, their religion was shown precisely by their inscription of an altar to an "unknown god." If religion is a way of dealing with the unknown, then, as knowledge increases the need for religion decreases. This

Bonhoeffer saw to be increasingly the situation in Western culture since the Enlightenment and the rise of modern science. When reference to God is used to fill in the gaps of our knowledge of the real world, as the gaps become less, this stop-gap God becomes less necessary. We see a carry-over of this usage today in insurance policies where the label "act of God" is applied only to damages for which no one can be held liable. It always refers to a disaster! In a "world come of age," Bonhoeffer writes, "there is no longer any need for God as a working hypothesis" used to explain what is otherwise unexplainable.[44] Not only is this a cultural fact as science advances, it is true to the Gospel's call to maturity in faith. Religion causes us to look for God in one direction, the mysterious unknown; the Gospel directs faith to look in another direction, to what happens with a slave on a cross confessed to have made God known. "No longer children tossed to and fro and blown about by every wind of doctrine," writes the author of Ephesians, "we are to grow up in every way unto him who is the head, into Christ" (Eph. 4.14-15).

We can certainly question today whether Bonhoeffer was right in thinking that the modern world's "coming of age" would mean that it would outgrow religion. Researchers have now documented approximately ten thousand different religions active on this planet, with two or three new ones thought to be emerging every day.[45] But with respect to religion, Bonhoeffer's position may most aptly be summed up in the words of Ephesians 4.20, "That is not the way you learned Christ!" The turn from the direction of religion, as Bonhoeffer sees it, does not mean a turning away from God's forthcoming from heaven, but just the opposite. Rather, as he later expresses it, it means "a clearing of the decks for the God of the Bible."[46] It also means facing reality.

2. Reality

Like the New Testament testimonies to which we have referred, Bonhoeffer depicted reality in an eventful frame of reference that spoke of the real as taking place — in his words, "taking form." The "real world" is said to be Christ "taking form" in all things. "The reality of Christ," Bonhoeffer writes, "comprises the reality of the world within itself."[47] Here we find a twentieth-century discussion of ethics articulated within a frame of reference informed by the Letter to the Colossians which speaks of "all things in heaven and on earth" as created and reconciled "in" Christ, "whether thrones or dominions or rulers or powers — all things have been created through him and for him" (Col. 1.15-20). What takes place with Christ is seen to be inclusive of all creation: all things are said to find their coherence, to "consist,"

Bonhoeffer writes, in this way (Col.1.17).[48] What is being said here is very different, Bonhoeffer contends, from our more familiar modern frame of reference which automatically assumes such language to be saying that Christianity, or religion, is somehow being viewed as taking over the world.

Yet the "real" in this sense, Bonhoeffer argues, can never be known abstracted from present-day events as a timeless moral law or general principle. It can only be realized in responding concretely to actual situations, for it comes to us as the Word made flesh. "What can and must be said," he writes, "is not what is good once and for all, but the way in which Christ takes form among us here and now."[49] This current "taking form" calls for recognizing "the significant in the factual."[50] Determining what love seeks as best in the here and now is always a concrete opportunity that calls for facing not only the facts of a situation, but what they are signifying. Merely keeping on a moral track already laid down and in place is, in Bonhoeffer's judgment, to miss following what is really taking place in our midst. He was astounded that Kant could reduce the morality of truth-telling to factual reporting without regard for its contextual significance.[51]

From his prison cell, surrounded by Gestapo guards who held his death sentence in their hands, Bonhoeffer left these words, "There is no part of the world, be it never so forlorn and never so godless, which is not accepted by God and reconciled with God in Jesus Christ. Whoever sets eyes on the body of Jesus Christ in faith can never again speak of the world as though it were lost, as though it were separated from Christ; [we] can never again with clerical arrogance set [ourselves] apart from the world. The world belongs to Christ, and it is only in Christ that the world is what it is . . . and . . . only in the midst of the world that Christ is Christ."[52]

These words from his final days are not inconsistent with things Bonhoeffer had first defended in his dissertation as a doctoral candidate when he wrote about Christ being present for us today in terms of social reality. But it is one thing to hear his testimony before an academic dissertation defense committee, and quite another to hear it before the gallows that are waiting for him in the courtyard just beyond his door.

3. *Responsibility*

If this is "the real world" of what God is doing, where does it leave the question of our human responsibility? For Bonhoeffer, it redefines it as the ability-to-respond in a way that is distinguishable from a law governed ethics (deontology), a goal directed ethics (teleology) or (utilitarianism), the application of the love command within changing situational constraints (situation ethics), and a derivative of virtue as anthropologically characterized (virtue ethics). *In short, responsibility for that over which we have control derives from the ability-to-respond to that which we do not control, namely the reality from heaven that is at hand.*[53] This ability to respond to reality, to what the concrete situation at hand calls for, comes not from our doing, but from the enabling power of that heavenly reality in the situation itself. What facing reality calls *for* the reality facing us calls *forth*.

"It is not Christian [individuals] who shape the world with their ideas," Bonhoeffer writes from prison, ". . . applying directly to the world the teaching of Christ or what are referred to as Christian principles, so that the world might be formed in accordance with these." On the contrary, it is Christ who does the shaping of us. ". . . Formation comes only by being drawn into the form of Jesus Christ. It comes only as formation in His likeness, as *conformation* with the unique form of Him who was made [human], was crucified, and rose again." This is not a formation that can be achieved, Bonhoeffer stresses, by what he calls "our efforts 'to become like Jesus'." Such self-effort represents a misplaced confidence that has no time to be for others. The ability-to-respond to what the actual situation at hand calls for, that kind of response-ability, he writes, comes "only when the form of Jesus Christ itself works upon us in such a manner that it moulds our form in its own likeness (Gal. 4.9)."[54] Because Christ is "Man for others," and deputizes his followers to be "for others," the forms of service this conformity with Christ takes are as varied, writes Bonhoeffer, as the others themselves. This means, Bonhoeffer concludes, "that though the form of Christ certainly is and remains one and the same, yet it is willing to take form in real [human beings], that is to say, in quite different guises."[55] The "voice of Christ," he had earlier written, encounters us precisely in "the foreignness [*Fremdartigkeit*]" of the other.[56]

A "Protestantism without Reformation," as Bonhoeffer sees it, is full of exhortation to become active and to take responsibility. It looks to the modern world as it seems and asks how it can find a relevant place for Jesus within it. A Reformation faith in "what God's word is doing" looks to Jesus and finds the whole world — with all its sin and godless godforsakenness — already there in what is taking place with him, thus discovering in what God is doing in reconciling the world in Christ the ability to respond in a participative freedom. The difference is between an ethical imperative to act and a faith actually empowered to act by a "form" of this-worldliness that is not the "form (*schema*) of this world that is passing away" (1 Cor. 7.31), of which Paul writes, but the new shaping of events made possible by the coming from heaven of the "Real One" (*der Wirkliche*) in whom, as Paul also writes, "God was reconciling the world" (2 Cor. 5.19). "The Sabbath was made for human beings, not human beings for the Sabbath" (Mk. 2.27). Undergirding these reflections is a hearing of the news of Gospel, "I, when I am lifted up . . . will draw all people to myself" (Jn 12.32).

Doing as in Heaven

Bonhoeffer's writings serve to highlight contrasting directions in ethical perspectives and bring to the fore disputed points and counterpoints with regard to the relation of divine and human agency in hearing the Gospel news of heaven. The themes just considered represent a distillation of only part of his ethical reflections, which were still incomplete at the time of his death, but they are among the most characteristic. Titles of such other works as *The Cost of Discipleship* (1937) and *Life Together* (1938) suggest how these themes were lived out and supplemented by a deep commitment to the spiritual disciplines of communal Bible study, participation in the sacraments, and prayer that guided his risky countercultural efforts in training pastors for the Confessing Church in its struggle for faithfulness to the Word of God in disbelieving the opposing Nazi racist influence of the so-called "German Christians."[57] The almost monastic concentration upon such spiritual discipline during the short period the Confessing seminaries were allowed to operate under the Third Reich earned Bonhoeffer the label by some of being more Catholic than Protestant in this regard and demonstrates that the distinction he draws of a Reformation church is not to be interpreted as sectarian.

A more comprehensive account of Bonhoeffer's ethics would also need to assess tensions in his arguments that leave questions still to be resolved. One has to do with the congruence of an ethics of commandment with an ethics of responsibility, both of which he advocates. How well Bonhoeffer's reflections about responsibility in the real world cohere with his emphasis upon the *commandment* of God must take into account his description of command as not only ordering, as we generally hear the term, but more especially as claiming, evoking, and permitting the freedom to act that, he writes, is "generated precisely by God's commandment."[58] This generative sense of command that calls *forth* what is called *for* is neither simply an obligation demanded nor a categorical imperative grounded in Kantian assumptions of moral autonomy.

A second tension is apparent between a more spatially delineated ontology of the Real (*der Wirkliche*) expressed in the discourse of communal formation and structure (*Gestalt*) in contrast to a more timely or eventful delineation of the Real usually associated with eschatology and closer to the apocalyptic parameters we have been considering of a heavenly inbreaking.[59]

On this second question of whether the more spatial nuances of Bonhoeffer's discourse about "form" and "structure" (*Gestalt*) result in a prioritizing of order over event or happening, his claims that the Christological direction of an "orientation from above to below" give warrant for affirming a hierarchical structure of "ethical authority" of the old over the young, the parent over the child, the master over the servant, the teacher over the student, the judge over the defendant, the governing authority over the subject, and the preacher over the parishioner have provoked perhaps the most criticism.[60] Though Bonhoeffer qualifies such a hierarchical ordering of authority by distinguishing it from any claim upon human beings affecting, in his words, "hunger, sexuality, or political power" that may arise from "the instinct for self-preservation" in "earthly powers and laws,"[61] it appears nonetheless to be clearly at odds with another more favorably quoted passage from 1942 in his *Letters and Papers from Prison* of "The View from Below," where he writes in the spirit of Luther's "theology of the cross" of learning "to see the great events of world history from below, from the perspective of the outcast, the suspects, the mal-treated, the powerless, the oppressed, the reviled — in short, from the perspective of those who suffer."[62]

On both these counts the later work of the theological ethicist Paul Lehmann, Bonhoeffer's close American friend and colleague at Union in the thirties, takes up the question of "what God is doing" and develops a more explicitly apocalyptic rendering of what Lehmann calls "the power and presence of Jesus of Nazareth in and over human affairs" and recasts the discussion of hierarchical authority in terms of a "reciprocal responsibility in heterogeneity" that Lehmann finds more in keeping with Bonhoeffer's major concerns.[63]

In the legacy of reflection we have been focusing upon, the emphasis has been on "what *God* is doing." What then may we conclude from these parameters about ethics as a characterization of *our* own human doing "as in heaven"?

In sum, the Enlightenment effort following Kant is shown to be one of de-activating claims of divine agency in order to activate human agency. This is an understandable move when political appeals to divine right are being used to deny human rights, but, as Johannes Weiss recognized yet felt unable to correct, it short circuits the Gospel's news of heaven's forthcoming direction and accordingly, in Weiss's judgment, must be said to result in a "thoroughly unbiblical" ethics. Reference to heaven is left out of the ethical equation with respect to moral responsibility or earthly doing on the assumption that it induces, as Kant puts it, our falling into "the indolence of awaiting from above, in passive leisure, what we should seek within." With no "real-world" envisagement of a kingdom now happening at hand, the mood shifts from the indicative to the imperative, and eschatological parables of the *basileia* from heaven are reduced to moral maxims leading to the "hortatory" character of the anthropologically grounded ethics that Martyn finds so contrary to the Apostle Paul. God can command our duty but is rendered incapable of doing more. As the ethicist Susan Owen observes, "The sinner Kant identifies cannot be assured by the God Kant allows."[64] Nor does the reascribing of agency from a theological *virtus* denoting an efficacious power of God's Spirit, as we have seen in Calvin, to an anthropological *virtue* within the power of human disposition, "up to us and voluntary," as Aristotle characterizes it, allow for a virtue ethics that is any more adequate than a deontological ethics in specifically this parabolic and apocalyptic regard.[65]

But if we confess to hearing in the news of the Gospel of a doing on earth that derives from a doing in heaven, and not the other way around, it matters decisively what the words "in heaven" are taken to mean and how tractable or intractable heaven is heard to be. Hearing of heaven as a transcendental moral norm, or as an hereafter at the end of time, or as a qualitative state, is not to hear of a contravening interruption of the *status quo* taking form and taking place in reality now at hand. "Persevere in the interruption" that "exceeds your perseverance;" "seize in your being that which has seized and broken you," writes the self-described atheist philosopher Alain Badiou, in a twenty-first century expression of "ethics" acknowledging Paul's declaration of the Gospel that would have confounded Weiss and the definers of "the modern Protestant world-view," but not Bonhoeffer.[66] This is not an ethics of a normative law defining legitimacy, a goal to be achieved, an ideal state, or an award in the hereafter. In contrast to the railroad to heaven, this interruption of an eventful reality that first seizes and claims us for fidelity to its truth is indeed a break in our tracks.

There is an imperative in hearing the declaratives in the Gospel news of heaven's forthcoming, a variously expressed summons to "watch," to "wait upon," to "seek first" its *basileia*, "to love one another," to "struggle" against the authorities and powers of this world's present darkness. In every case the imperative is generated by the promise seizing the moment of what is at hand. "Watch" — for your redemption is drawing near (Lk. 21.28). "Wait upon" the Lord — for the Lord will renew your strength (Isa. 40.31). "Seek first the kingdom" — for it is the Father in heaven whose good pleasure it is to give it to you (Mt. 6.33; Lk. 12.32). "Love one another" — for you have first been loved (1 Jn 4.19). "Struggle" against the current powers of darkness — for with the shield of faith you will be able to quench all the flaming arrows of the evil one (Eph. 6.12, 16). Finally, having done all "to stand" — for you are now seated with Christ in the heavenly places (Eph. 6.13; 2.6). In such a hearing our facing of the future is empowered by the reality of the future that is facing us, not abstractly, but concretely in our multiple circumstances, by a perseverance in a freedom of grace expressed in the paradox of Paul's words, "I worked . . . though it was not I, but the grace of God that is with (*syn*) me" (1 Cor. 15.10), a synergistic doing neither autonomous nor on automatic pilot.

Both Badiou and Calvin write of an ethics of "perseverance" deriving from a "grace" to continue in fidelity to a truth event that, in Badiou's words, like the Resurrection Paul declares, "exceeds perseverance." For Calvin, this is God's providential grace, said to be of Christ's heavenly, immeasurable *virtus*. For Badiou, with an atheist resistance to any hint of divine calculation or unearthly transcendence — and ignoring that it is arguably the Gospel news of *heaven's* parabolic and apocalyptic *at-handedness* which disallows both! — this is a nameless "laicized grace," said to be of incalculable "chance."[67] For each, strikingly enough, as for Bonhoeffer, it is an anti-moralistic characterization of "getting what is coming to us" as other than our just deserts that is said to be the generative factor in our ethical doing.

Chapter 5

THE HOPE OF HEAVEN

It is doubtful if any subject in human history has been more associated with human hopes than the subject of heaven. Yet it is also the case that the thought of heaven can be the occasion for fear, a foreboding of the unknown future, an anxiety of not making it, or, as we say, not getting to heaven, but of life arriving instead as a lost soul or mere shadow of the self at that dreaded portal made famous by Dante's words in Canto III of the *Inferno*, "Abandon all hope, all ye who enter here." To trace the long history of what the hearing of heaven brings to mind is to find claims of piety that the hope of heaven requires the disregard of earth, and equally insistent claims of secularity that the hope of earth, and our responsibility for it, requires the disregard of heaven. Kant to his credit tried to give due deference to some validity in both concerns by relocating heaven's access in morality rather than in metaphysics, a move Johannes Weiss recognized as unbiblical, but saw no modern alternative except to change the subject. The parameters of the foregoing pages rule out both contentions, as well as the direction of Kant's attempted relocation, but to what hope of heaven do these parameters, we must now ask, bear witness?

From the four preceding chapters we thus come back now to the simple question that has instigated this inquiry: So what? It is for any claims regarding heaven the most demanding question of all. Whether the trajectory of deliberations and the terminologies of the discourses we have been following have been familiar ground or foreign territory, and whether beckoning or baffling, in Emily Dickinson's words, the issue finally comes down to what difference, if any, it all really makes.

Mindful of Jesus' admonition that those who come seeking bread not be given a stone (Mt. 7.9), when all is said and done, what hope is there, what "very present help," in this hearing of the Gospel testimony of heaven? To recall the words of the Psalmist: "Our help is in the name of the Lord, who made heaven and earth" (Ps. 124.8); "God is our refuge and strength, a very present help in trouble" (Ps. 46.1). Such hope and help must be more than a theoretical abstraction.

The most comprehensive minds in the history of Christian theology have attested to theology's limitations. Augustine, who never hesitated to confess, "I am at a loss to understand," when attending to the mystery of heaven, concludes his monumental treatise on *The City of God*, over which he had labored from 413 to 426, with the plea, "Let those who think I have said too little, or those who think I have said too much, forgive me; and let those who think I have said just enough give thanks, not to me, but rather join me in giving thanks to God. Amen."[1]

When in 1273 Thomas Aquinas reportedly was asked by his faithful and concerned assistant, Reginald of Piperno, why, after fifteen years of daily writing and dictation covering virtually every conceivable issue of Christian teaching in more than forty volumes he had so abruptly stopped after an experience while celebrating mass and refused to continue, Thomas is said to have replied, "Reginald, I cannot. All that I have written seems to me like straw compared to what has now been revealed to me."[2]

Closer to our own time, no less a theologian than Karl Barth, whose prodigious accomplishment has been compared to that of Thomas, in his last series of lectures commented upon how the undertaking of theology is always assailed by the thought of the disparity that exists between what it discusses and "the sea of suffering and misery prevailing in the world that surrounds [it]." *There* in the midst of the world, as Barth expresses it, is "the madness of dictators . . . the murderers and the murdered of concentration camps . . . Hiroshima, Korea, Algeria, the Congo . . . the undernourishment of the greater part of humanity . . . the stubbornly promoted end of all life on our planet . . . [While] *here*, however, in the realm of theology, is a little de-mythologizing in Marburg and a little *Church Dogmatics* in Basle . . . the rediscovery of 'the historical Jesus' and [some] glorious new discovery of the 'God above God,' . . . discussions on baptism and eucharist, Law and Gospel, Kerygma and myth . . . ecumenical Church councils. Nothing of all this should be underestimated, much less disparaged," Barth concluded. "But *Kyrie Eleison!* — what is the real relationship to everything that simultaneously [is happening] *there*?"[3]

Or, to quote a satirical remark in lighter vein from a popular novel that no doubt speaks for many, "'I know nothing about theology,' said Mrs. Cobden-Smith . . . 'I always say . . . that I know nothing about theology and I don't want to know anything either. As far as I'm concerned, God's God, the Church is the Church, the Bible's the Bible and I can't understand what all the arguments are about.'"[4]

If the argument is really about what is nearest to us, its point is elemental. It brings us back to basics. The first cry of the newborn emerging from the spasms of the mother's womb signals entry into a world where two facts are certain. The time and space occupied by this life and all its relationships, whether long or short, near or far, will be uniquely its own, unduplicated by any other in the vast reaches of all creation. And in this world there will be tribulation (Jn 16.33). Why this is so, or why in the second instance it could not have been otherwise, we do not know, and the learned arguments that presume to explain it all theoretically by way of a theodicy inevitably fail to convince. How hearing of heaven relates to these facts of our knowing and unknowing, and the hope that attends it, is the subject now before us. For to these two facts it poses yet a third to be reckoned with, denoted as *Gospel*, which, taken in the context of its full import, means nothing less than the best news anyone could ever hear.

Up to this point we have been focusing on hearing this news of heaven's nearness that is said to be *at hand*, an occurrence of proximity currently taking place, but in a decisive contrast to the form of the world presently established and in place within our capacity for control and approximation; in short, what in this respect may be said to be *in hand*. Now, when we ask, "what is the best news one could ever hear as the Gospel proclaims it?" we are led in a third consideration to speak of being *on hand* for heaven. Our everyday talk of being on hand, and not being on hand, expresses some of our deepest longings and our most persistent fears.

Why Should We Not Be Afraid?

No hearing of the Gospel can fail to be struck by one of its most constantly reiterated messages, "Do not be afraid."[5] Yet the Gospel accounts make no attempt to disguise the sorts of things that most cause us to fear. Tribulation on both an external and internal scale is not glossed over, denied, or made to seem less horrific than what the Psalmist calls "the terror of the night . . . and the destruction that wastes at noonday" (Ps. 91.5-6). "Daughters of Jerusalem, do not weep for me, but for yourselves and for your children," are words remembered by the early church of Jesus on his way to the cross. "For the days are surely coming when they will say, 'Blessed are the barren,

and the wombs that never bore, and the breasts that never nursed.'
Then they will begin to say to the mountains, 'Fall on us'; and to the
hills, 'Cover us'" (Lk. 23.28-30). Critics of much heaven talk rightly
point out how easily it becomes the projection of our thwarted desires,
the desperate attempts at a detour from having to face in our own time
and space the worst of life's dead ends. "Heaven comes down to earth
as a pleasant neighborhood that reflects the society that produced it"
is a newspaper headline in 2003 announcing that eighty-two percent
of Americans say they believe in heaven, the one factor of religious
increase while most others are in decline.[6] This percentage to date in
polling remains virtually unchanged. Yet to hear in the Gospel the hope
of heaven is at the same time to hear of a cry of god-forsakenness at the
heart of this news which, despite all the veneer of our sentimentality and
wishful thinking, will not relent to being covered up by the narcotics of
our pleasantries (Mk 15.34, Mt. 27.46, Ps. 22.1). "The end of all things
is at hand," are words from 1 Peter. "Beloved, do not be surprised at
the fiery ordeal that is taking place among you to test you, as though
something strange were happening to you" (1 Pet. 4.7, 12).

1. *Facing What Is Not Within Our Hands*

Our greatest fear is being left with loss, whatever form it takes. We
dread a loss of freedom, security, interest, strength and health, reputa-
tion, memory, landmarks, friends, even looks. Feared most of all is
the loss of life; that of loved ones, and our own. In every case it is the
finality of sooner or later having to face what we have no power to
remedy or to reverse, what is not within our hands, that may make us
most afraid. I am told that, as a child who was only seven months old
when his father died, when in the company of other children who spoke
of their dads I would announce, as if to bridge somehow a connection
with them, "My father has gone to heaven." A single photograph on
my bedside table through the years has been my silent reminder, once
seeming old, now young to me, but always to my often questioning
look unrelentingly, as gone and away — in "the land beyond the river,
that we call the sweet forever," as the old revival hymn goes that I was
told they sang at his funeral. "One by one we'll gain the portals," the
hymn continues, "there to dwell with the immortals, when they ring
the golden bells for you and me."[7] It is not Dante, but it follows in the
same direction. Of my father, who left a good name and was known for
his generosity, the preacher at his coffin had uttered words commending
him and his spirit, saying, "All that he now holds in his cold hands is
what he has given away." It was a stark committal, meant for comfort
for a young widow and an unknowing infant, intended perhaps, in

Dickinson's words, as a "twig of evidence" that some virtue in hand could assure one's hope of gaining access to the heavenly *virtus* of portals beyond. An accustomed twig to be sure, but in hearing the news of heaven at hand not a branch from the vine of life (Jn 15.5).

Emily Dickinson's words prove a stern companion for talk of heaven's hope: "Narcotics cannot still the tooth that nibbles at the soul." The seminar on heaven and hell in Christian testimony that early on provided initial spade work leading to these eventual reflections had its first session scheduled for 10 a.m., September 11, 2001. Having not yet learned of the terrorist attacks earlier that morning on the World Trade Center towers downtown, and of the canceling of all the seminary's classes, several students arrived, one quickly leaving in fright to check on her child in daycare, another turning to say to me earnestly in heading out the door, "How could anyone *not* believe in hell?" The nibbling of the soul can cut deep, as readers of these pages will attest. Purveyors of false hope come under prophetic condemnation in the scriptures for the crimes against humanity that they foster by treating the wounds of people carelessly, saying, "Peace, peace, when there is no peace" (Jer. 6.14). We are forewarned.

Out of town, away from school one Christmas day, on a break from preparing a lecture on "the real world," I took brief leave from the usual festive time with family and friends around the dinner table to make two hospital visits to see relatives unable to be with us. One visit was to an Alzheimer's unit where a ninety-four-year-old relative stared blankly at me, as she had on the previous three Christmases. For years we always went to mid-night Christmas Eve communion services together, and on Christmas mornings at her home she led the family in champagne toasts served elegantly in silver goblets. But now all elegance is gone, and when I leave the room I hear her ask, "Who was that?"

The other visit was across town in the neo-natal wing of a children's hospital, where a young niece, whose marriage I had performed, had gone every day since mid-August to sit by an incubator and touch her infant son, born some twelve weeks prematurely, and still on life-support. The infant by now had gained from the various tubes attached, almost seven pounds to this point, up from the one and a half pounds at birth. But he cannot swallow yet, and he cannot cry, and on this Christmas day the nurses report that there is, again, still another infection. He had not long to live. I put my hand on his head. "We have named him Christian," the mother tells me.

Coming back from these two visits, the question mocks and gnaws: What is "the real world" in each of these circumstances where, at both ends of "the life cycle," as we say, life struggles so desperately to conclude and to begin? And what of afflictions on a more massive scale, multiplied disasters causing untold deprivations? Is not theological talk about "heaven at hand" as *life that is coming to us* but a pretentious denial of these worlds and of those who inhabit them? Such sites of life and death, we dare neither forget nor exploit, are the inescapable locales at ground level testing all forecasts of hope. There will come times we cannot read, argue, or care, and yet we still are told, "Be not afraid."

2. *Witnessing Heaven*

Faced with such concrete instances of tribulation, can the parameters as we have traced them really be said to bear true witness to the hope of heaven? Does not the news of heaven as a taking-place at hand seem a pale reflection indeed before a richer panoply flush with golden bells, identifiable angels, and scenic glimpses imagined of depicted saints in activity beyond the river affording a greater visibility of Dickinson's "species that waits beyond," with or without its census records already foreordained? We have earlier noted Badiou's observation that the heaven in keeping with Paul's declaration of the Resurrection registers neither with the calculations of those demanding signs nor of those seeking wisdom.

Most attempts to visualize heaven's hope have in fact focused on the more common associations of heaven with the sky, the hereafter, or a state of bliss.[8]

A theologian friend impressed by a recent biography of Cicero (106–43 BC) which portrayed him as "Rome's greatest politician," has reminded me that, while being noted for commending civic virtue, Cicero also recalls Plato's philosophy that a dissociation of ourselves from our bodies and public affairs prepares us as an earthly divestment for a heavenly life. Like others before him, Cicero reports the dream of a virtuous life as a highway to a heavenly meeting of reward in the stars, not visible from such a tiny dot as earth, but above the moon and Milky Way where everything is eternal. My friend, observing that this would probably fit well with the views of many Christians, attaches a note: "I take it the heaven you envision is different"![9]

The Roman Catholic theologian John Thiel makes an insightful case for a more "thick description" of heavenly life, or what he calls simply "the *eschata*," meaning last things. For him the eschatological imagination is directed not toward the sky but toward heaven as a postmortem afterlife.[10] Thiel gently suggests that the reformers, as well as Kant, are responsible for clamping down the eschatological imagination of heaven as the life hereafter of the blessed dead by their decrying of the veneration of the saints as idolatry and thereby denying any depiction of an ongoing activity of discipleship and participation in Christ's ministry of reconciliation following death. There is not much "doing" for the reformers on "those endless Sabbaths the blessed ones see."[11] He jokingly advises, in response to my own confessed concerns about too parsimonious a celestial imagination — too "thin" by his descriptive standards — "maybe a bit more tilt in the direction of Catholic kitsch!"

In an illuminating article, "For What May We Hope? Thoughts on the Eschatological Imagination," that I by no means consider "kitsch," Thiel spells out his position that the blessed dead (no unblessed dead are mentioned) can be envisioned as actively continuing their discipleship in imitating Christ's reconciling work as exemplified in the resurrection appearances in the Gospel. Taking the influential theologian of Vatican II, Karl Rahner's, starting point of the self and its quest for transcendence, but diverging from what he takes to be Rahner's too-close affinity with Kant's strictures on imagining the beyond, Thiel argues that for the blessed dead to retain their identity and to be themselves "they must continue to be persons shaped" by their history, which means in this instance "the history of sin," the burden which "they have both made and suffered." As such they may be imagined in the afterlife as still pursuing the "negotiation" to defeat this sinful burden by actively participating in Christ's acts of reconciliation. This he finds more in keeping with the imaginative robustness of traditional Catholic imagery regarding the hereafter. Without such a postmortem continuance of their *imatatio Christi* in acts "that defeat the burden of sin that they both made and suffered," and which "the exercise of character demands," the blessed, in Thiel's view, would lose their "integrity" of "being themselves" with historically constituted identities as "persons shaped by the history of sin." Thiel's cogent reflections, which are focused on heaven as a hereafter and not on a forthcoming *basileia* from heaven at hand, provide an instructive alternative to the parabolic and apocalyptic envisionment and engagement discussed in these pages.

Such a portrayal of the *eschata*, Thiel acknowledges, may indeed sound more like "an account of life in purgatory," which the reformers rejected as contrary to the news of the Gospel, "than of heavenly life."[12] The delineation imagined is of a past, identified by the historicity of its burden in sin, continuing to be readied toward a future of greater good. It is not of an apocalypse, or taking place, now at hand but not in hand of a new creation.

In yet another insightfully articulated account, titled *Undiscovered Country: Imagining the World to Come*, the Dante scholar Peter S.

Hawkins demonstrates the power and pertinence of Dante's poetic vision that, like Thiel's conceptual proposal, views heaven depicted as *Paradiso* from the standpoint of the human quest in its purification toward higher realms of beatitude and bliss. Like Thiel, Hawkins finds a more purgatorial relevance and realism in Dante's vision for our present time. "It has to be said . . . that most readers of the third canticle are not entirely ecstatic over the result. They miss the excitement of *Inferno* and the sense of becoming new that is found in *Purgatorio* — in other words, miss the poignant encounters with lost souls or with those who are works-in-progress like us."[13] Again, in this tracking of heaven the direction envisioned is of a paradise of bliss to be journeyed toward by a work-in-progress, as distinguished from an inbreaking state of affairs forthcoming from heaven into our midst at hand and off track in the sense that this coming of life toward us does not approximate any form of worldly life that we hear Paul call "perishable" and "passing away." "What I am saying, brothers and sisters, is this," Paul writes in his first Letter to the Corinthians, "flesh and blood cannot inherit the kingdom of God, nor does the perishable inherit the imperishable." The context is Paul's message regarding what he calls "the mystery" of being changed from bearing the image of the first Adam, or "man (*anthropos*) from dust," to bearing the image of the second Adam, or Christ, as the "man (*anthropos*) from heaven" (1 Cor. 15.49-51). If it follows from what we are hearing that an anthropology of heavenly life cannot be accommodated by an anthropology of perishable life — i.e. by any prior world *schema* that is passing away — then images of the earthly historicity of the self do not carry over into heavenly identities as analogues of character development, as Thiel's reference to what "the exercise of character demands" implies. Rather, the word is of nothing less radical than "a new creation" (2 Cor. 5.17), what the Fourth Gospel relates as "heavenly things" in Jesus telling Nicodemus that entrance into the *basileia* of God is by being "born *anōthen*" (ἄνωθεν), meaning both "born anew" and "born from above" (Jn 3.3, 7).

The acknowledgement by both Thiel and Hawkins of a more purgatorial realism suggested in imagined quests for heaven that are focused upon the hereafter calls to mind the anxiety that was at the heart of the Reformation debates about whether "the great transaction's done," as an eighteenth-century hymn once popular in evangelical circles expresses it,[14] or whether some further "negotiation," in Thiel's words, may still be required depending upon what one holds at death in one's cold hands.[15]

The lineaments of the Gospel depictions of heaven vary and, as was said in the beginning, there is no single uniform view. Among the scriptural witnesses we do hear references to heaven as the sky, life after death, or a state of bliss, references deeply engrained in our consciousness that have parallels in many ancient traditions. These historically have been the subjects of most heavenly imaginings. But it is striking that none of these is given the priority in the Gospel testimonies that is given to the news of life from heaven that is now coming to us as a new state of affairs said to be at hand. This heaven neither begins nor ends with death. It is this news of heaven's *at-handedness*, variously expressed as the course of God's forthcoming, as creation and new creation, as a present community or *politeia*, and as a kingdom or dominion, a *basileia*, that may be said to provide the context or frame of reference for whatever else we hear of heaven in the Gospel message. According to this news, the *at-handedness* of heaven, as we have observed, is parabolically signified and apocalyptically realized, which simply means that it is conveyed in the Gospel in the form of parables and said to be apocalypsed; that is, "revealed" as real not by what is in place and passing away, but by what is taking place and newly coming to pass.

An example of eschatological imagination that focuses not on the sky or on the afterlife but on heaven's inbreaking in current affairs may be found in Paul Lehmann's theological ethics, as previously mentioned in connection with Bonhoeffer.[16] Writing in light of the social turmoil of 1968, Lehmann refers to lines often quoted from the poet William Butler Yeats, among them,

> Things fall apart; the centre cannot hold;
> Mere anarchy is loosed upon the world . . .
> Surely some revelation is at hand;
> Surely the Second Coming is at hand . . .

Lehmann observes that for Yeats the news of a coming "at hand" is heard not as an occasion for hope but as a reminder of troubles that portend:

> The darkness drops again; . . .
> And what rough beast, its hour come round at last,
> Slouches towards Bethlehem to be born?[17]

To discern the Gospel witness to this coming *at-handedness*, Lehmann's approach is to attend specifically to both the parabolic and apocalyptic aspects of the Gospel testimonies by drawing upon the juxtapositions that we hear in the Gospel and find echoed in the troubles of the day, what he calls in a note on parabolic significance, "juxtapositions of the incommensurable." He writes, "For a *parable*, at least in the biblical sense, has to do with an imaginative juxtaposition of what is incommensurable, namely, the way of God and the ways of man [our human ways]."[18]

This witnessing of the news of heaven's *at-handedness* suggests a different kind of depiction from that of imagining heaven as in the sky or as the hereafter of the blessed dead.

3. *Juxtapositions of the Incommensurable*

To hear the Gospel is to hear news of its central figure, Jesus, said to be identified with God's eternal life and our own, going away where we cannot come, and vanishing out of sight, juxtaposed with news of his being with us always, never separated from us, and never leaving us orphaned, apart from him. What may appear on the surface — or what Paul calls "according to fleshly appearances," meaning "according to our familiar ways of looking at things" (*kata sarka*) — to be a message neither here nor there may also be heard as news that the *there* of heaven is *here* without ceasing to be *there*. In what sense this may be said to make sense and be more than a mere abstraction or play on words is what we have been inquiring into in noting that the Gospel's proclamation of Jesus' kingdom as not *from* this world but as coming *to* this world is parabolically signified and apocalyptically realized as heavenly life taking place now at hand. As witnessed parabolically, what may initially sound like contradictions are not heard literalistically as univocally commensurate signs, the sort of "Lo, here" and "Lo, there" equally observable happenings that the Gospel teaching of Jesus warns against believing (Mk 13.21), but as what we have seen Barth term "saga," that, in Calvin's words, comes to our hearing "vested in promise." In short, the Gospel witness of heaven takes expression in juxtapositions that are not commensurate but incommensurate. In this respect it speaks of hope and "very present help" without denial of the conditions causing our deepest fears.

We may take, as four examples, losses not merely theoretical, but personally and concretely experienced as most dreaded and profound: the losses of security, of strength, of freedom, and of life itself.

The more cosmic sense of the loss of worldly security, commonly associated with textual accounts deemed apocalyptic, is evidenced in the fear and foreboding of what is coming upon the world described in the synoptic accounts of Matthew 24.29-31, Mark 13.24-27, and Luke 21.9-36, to whose more detailed version I refer. In the context of speaking about such tribulations in terms tragically familiar to many as earthquakes, plagues, famines, and persecutions, Jesus' words as reported tell of "distress on the earth among nations confused by the roaring of the sea and the waves, people faint from fear and foreboding of what is coming upon the world for the powers of the heavens will be shaken." No attempt is made to deny the "dreadful portents" of such catastrophic loss of all worldly security of things presently in place. The losses referred to here are of the sort said not to be within the hands of the hearers to remedy or to reverse, leading some modern critics to reject such scriptural references in today's world as counsels of irresponsibility. Yet, juxtaposed to what on the surface certainly appears to be a fatalistic prediction entailing passivity before such overwhelming odds, we hear exactly the opposite: "Now when these things begin to take place, stand up and raise your heads, because your redemption is drawing near . . . Be on guard so that your hearts are not weighed down with dissipation and drunkenness and the worries of this life, . . . Be alert at all times, praying for the strength . . . to stand" before the future's coming, described — with allusion to the vision of the coming future named in Daniel 7.13-14 — as 'the Son of Man coming in a cloud' with power and great glory." In sum, when faced with having to endure the worst things that could possibly "come on all who live on the face of the earth," as Luke records it, the word we hear is, "But not a hair of your head will perish. By your endurance you will gain your souls." Clearly, how we hear of perishing is not univocal or commensurate in these Gospel juxtapositions.

In an equally universal but more individual sense, the fear of loss of physical strength with the endangerment of wellbeing also finds articulation in the news of the Gospel. Instances abound in the Hebrew scriptures, and Paul's apocalyptic testimony about new creation from heaven at hand does not serve as a denial of such tribulation. After recounting to the Corinthians his being "on frequent journeys, in danger from rivers, danger from bandits, danger from my own people, danger from Gentiles, danger in the city, danger in the wilderness, danger at sea, danger from false brothers and sisters, in toil and hardship, through many a sleepless night, hungry and thirsty, often without food, cold and naked, and besides other things . . . under daily pressure because of my anxiety for the churches" (2 Cor. 11.23-28), his acknowledgement in the same letter of what is plainly obvious, that "our outer nature is wasting away," comes as a bit of an understatement indeed. But what is definitely not equally obvious or visible to the eye is Paul's immediately juxtaposed claim that "our inner nature is being renewed day by day." "So we do not lose heart," he tells his hearers — who surely then and now after hearing Paul's list of tribulations must question if they have cause to complain about anything! — "because we look not at what can be seen but at what cannot be seen . . ."(2 Cor. 4.16-18). The visual imagery of "looking" at "what cannot be seen" provides a graphic instance of incommensurable juxtaposition. It also expresses what Paul writes elsewhere about hope: "Now hope that is seen is not hope" (Rom. 8.24).

The loss of freedom in both its world-historical and individual dimensions also confronts us in the hearing of the Gospel, where Rachel's refusal to be comforted, exemplified by her death in childbearing and also by the loss of her people, Israel, taken into captivity in Babylon, is juxtaposed with the promise given to her in Jeremiah, "There is hope for your future says the Lord" (Jer. 31.17). Incorporating Rachel's refusal of consolation into the angel's news of a coming "Emmanuel," or "God-With-Us," on the occasion of the Christ-child's birth, Matthew's Gospel gives Rachel's undeniable weeping over the slaughter of innocent life at Herod's command iconic status by the juxtaposition of the sound of her voice — recalled in the words of Genesis 35.19 as entombed "on the way to Bethlehem" — with proximity to "the place where the child was" (Mt. 1.20-23; 2.9, 16-18).[19]

The world-historical dimension of freedom's loss and its tragic human consequences unmistakably presents itself in hearing the Gospel references to slavery. Undeniable is the fact that household codes of social inequity familiar to the ancient world and consistent with Aristotle's "natural slave theory," that society by its nature was dependent upon the slavery of some for the greater good of all, is operative among the original hearers in the communities to which the Gospel is addressed.[20] Paul's brief Letter to Philemon, appealing to Philemon as the master of a deserted slave Onesimus, who has cared for Paul during his imprisonment, to "welcome him" back as "my own heart" and "as you would welcome me," "no longer as a slave but more than a slave, a beloved brother," assumes this social structure (Philemon, vs. 12, 16-17). According to Aristotle, this prevailing condition of servitude was not an unjust denial of freedom to those so enslaved so long as they were treated with due regard for their rights afforded them by their "nature," since all strata of society — husbands, wives, children, masters, and servants — were to keep within their "natural" place. The long course of this slave world's continuance and its tragic effects can be traced to the slave trades of modern times, and theology itself historically has been among the defenders most complicit in justifying its perpetuation.[21] For centuries it is virtually the exceptional voice of Gregory of Nyssa (c. 330–c.395) that stands out from the majority in refusing to make theological excuses for treating human beings as property.[22] In this instance the message, "Slaves, obey your earthly masters," a familiar hortatory admonition in the ancient world that one would expect to hear from upholders of the established order then in place, is juxtaposed with an announcement of heaven that could only have come (and still come!) as breaking news to those in positions of mastery assembled for its hearing: "And, masters . . . know that both of you have the same Master in heaven, and with him there is no partiality" (Eph. 6.5, 9).

From the Fourth Gospel, words reported of the Risen Christ to Peter describe a common dread of an individual loss of freedom, beyond simply indicating, as the text suggests, the early church remembered, Peter's coming death to the glory of God: "When you were younger, you used to fasten your own belt and to go wherever you wished. But when you grow old, you will stretch out your hands, and someone else will fasten a belt around you and take you where you do not wish to go" (Jn 21.18). This common and pervasive fear of a personal loss of freedom, of being taken where we do not wish to go in growing old, is not denied or covered up, but rather juxtaposed with hearing, in the words of Ephesians, that we are to "grow up in every way into him who is the head, into Christ . . ." (Eph. 4.5). What is presented as so plainly incommensurate in this juxtaposition is that the "growing up" as heard of here is of a growing from a past of death in the direction of coming life, precisely the reverse of an undeniably observable "growing old" from a past of living in the direction of coming death. "You were dead," so the Letter to the Ephesians quite abruptly announces when heard aloud (as it originally was in the early communities), "all of us," "having no hope," and yet — and here is the news — "even when dead through our trespasses, made . . . alive together with Christ . . . and raised . . . with him . . . in the heavenly places" (Eph. 2.1, 4-6). All this the writer, whether Paul or a close associate writing in his name, attributes to "the power at work within us — or 'among us,' ἐν ἡμῖν — [that] is able to accomplish abundantly far more than all we can ask or imagine" (Eph. 3.20).

Where losses of security, of strength, and of freedom in their public and private dimensions define "the terror of the night and the destruction that wastes at noonday," they reach their culmination in the fear of death and loss of life, "the last enemy to be destroyed," so writes Paul to the Corinthians (1 Cor. 15.26). And in this fourth instance no examples of the juxtapositions of incommensurability sound more existentially immediate and pronounced in hearing the Gospel today than the reports of what happens at Bethany (Lk. 10.38-42; Jn 11.1-44, 12.1-8).

Denials of Death at the Arrival of Life:
the News from Bethany

The scene as related is the outskirts of Jerusalem, a small village named Bethany, said to be within short walking distance from the city, just a couple miles away. Here, so we are told, two sisters, Martha and Mary, live at home with their brother Lazarus. Upon watching their brother grow ill and die, with all efforts to save his life unavailing and Jesus not coming at the time that they called for him, we hear the cry of the two grief-stricken sisters, "Lord, if you had been here, my brother would not have died." Their cry denies that death would have occurred if Jesus' arrival had been in time with Lazarus' passing away. As if to emphasize how individual the anguish is at the loss of a loved one's life, even when it is a shared grief, the identical words are repeated twice, spoken separately by each sister in turn (Jn 11.21, 32). It would be hard to find words in the New Testament which sound more realistic than the words of this cry. Their sentiment is echoed whenever all petitioning for help at the prospect of the loss of a loved one's life proves unavailing, and the sheer anguish of pleading, lament, and reproach that God — or whatever powers there be — could let this happen faces the unrelenting finality of the grave. It is a cry certainly not out of the range of many.

The reports from Bethany in Luke and John may be analyzed exegetically from a number of angles. Here the concern is with how they may resound today, with what in their current hearing sounds most familiar as being true to life as we know it and, juxtaposed against this, what sounds least so. We may best do this by focusing attention upon the juxtaposition of the two cries we hear uttered upon the arrival of Jesus at the tomb of Lazarus: the cry of the sisters and the cry of Jesus. The news of Jesus' cry is given in the Gospel account as follows: ". . . He cried out with a loud voice, 'Lazarus, come forth (δεῦρο ἔξω, 'come out here'). The dead man came out, his hands and feet bound with strips of cloth, and his face wrapped in a cloth. Jesus said to them, 'Unbind him, and let him go'" (Jn 11.43-44).

1. *The Cry of Martha and Mary*

If we listen to the conflated reports of Luke and John regarding the news from Bethany with an ear for the juxtaposition of these two cries, we are first introduced as background to the profiles of the two sisters and what they are characterized as bringing to their call upon Jesus to act in time to deny death their brother. Martha brings her work of much serving. Mary brings her attentive devotion. But a deeper significance to their interactions with Jesus becomes apparent at the tomb than a mere stereotyping suggests. As we hear of them, Martha and Mary, while residing in the same house with their brother, and equally grief-stricken in repeating the same cry in the face of death, are described as coming, as we tend to say, from very different places.

Martha is introduced in Luke's narrative as the one who is the first to welcome Jesus as a guest into their home as he passes on his way through Bethany. Generations no doubt have identified with the description Luke gives of Martha as someone occupied with much serving and having to do all the work by herself, with no help from others, to the point of being, as the reported words of Jesus describe her when visiting the home, "distracted by her many tasks" (Lk. 10.40). Martha is also the first to go out to greet Jesus upon word of his approaching arrival in the vicinity, and someone who just as hurriedly is said to return to inform her sister Mary in privacy back at home that "the Teacher is here and is calling for you" (Jn 11.28).

Mary, in decided contrast, is described as more retiring within the home. On one occasion when Jesus is in residence, we are told that she "sat at his feet and listened to what he was saying," so much so that Martha asks, "Lord, do you not care that my sister has left me to do all the work by myself? Tell her then to help me" (Lk. 10.39-40). On another occasion, at dinner when Martha is again said to be doing all the serving, John's Gospel reports that Mary pours expensive perfume on Jesus' feet, wiping them with her hair, and filling the whole house with fragrance (Jn 12.2-3). Yet, acting together, we are told, the sisters with both their characteristic ways of relating to Jesus, summon him with the message, "Lord, he whom you love is ill." To this summons the report is that when Jesus heard it, he said, "This illness does not lead to death; rather it is for God's glory," with John's Gospel adding, "Accordingly, though Jesus loved Martha and her sister and Lazarus, after having heard that Lazarus was ill, he stayed two days longer in the place where he was" (Jn 11.3-6).

When Jesus finally does come, it is four days too late according to the time of Lazarus' passing away. Many have come to console the sisters. What we are told is that, "When Martha heard that Jesus was coming, she went and met him" with her cry, "Lord, if you had been here . . .," while Mary, "stayed at home" (Jn 11.17-21). Whether we hear of Martha's outgoing activity or of Mary's more private devotion the sense conveyed of these sisters' attempt to deny death the loss of their brother in passing away is not difficult to imagine. Both are existential places and responses not unfamiliar to the passing away of life as we know it.

If treated as a morality play involving mere stereotypes of an active versus a more pious and passive role model, Martha's complaint about her sister sounds quite reasonable. It is in specific response to Martha's request for help that we hear the reply of Jesus: "Martha, Martha, you are worried and distracted by many things; there is need of only one thing. Mary has chosen the better part, which will not be taken away from her" (Lk. 10.41-42).

Heard with a moralistic ear according to our common standards of fair play, as with other accounts of Jesus' comments in the Gospels, it is a stunning rebuke, and generations identifying with Martha in having to do the actual work of waiting on others, whether at home or elsewhere, have objected to what sounds like an obvious case of domestic injustice. While interpreters hasten to point out that the honor Jesus gives to Mary's listening and devotion sheds favorable light upon the place of women among his early followers, even when criticized by the other disciples, as in the case of Judas, whom Jesus tells to "leave her alone" (Jn 12.4-7), and that it thereby speaks as well to the expanded context of life in the early church by stressing the priority for listening to the Gospel over a kind of works righteousness, the unfavorable treatment of Martha when framed as a matter of moral judgment still sounds disrespectful and unfair.

As with the previously considered incidents of Jesus' seemingly unfair cursing of a fig tree for not bearing fruit when it was not even the season for figs (Mk 11.12-14) — the incident that provoked the moral indignation of Bertrand Russell — and of the healing of the man with the withered hand that was seen to be in moral violation of established Sabbath observance (Lk. 6.6-11), this initial commonsense reaction of moral objection may alert us to the possibility that perhaps we are missing a more operative frame of reference in the Gospel reporting of the interactions in Bethany, and to that extent are failing to get the picture of what is taking place.

This only becomes clearer when we notice that Martha's *request is for help in a situation she herself describes as one of being left to do all the work by herself.* It is this same request in her complaint to Jesus with respect to her sister Mary having left her with all the work to do that is later intimated in her cry to Jesus with respect to her brother Lazarus having left her in death, with Jesus not seeming to care about all she had tried to do — all the serving, summoning, coming to meet him, whatever. In both instances the sense we may get from Martha is that of someone taking matters into her own hands and ending up being left without help, all alone.

2. The Arrival of Jesus at the Tomb of Lazarus

This appears to be borne out by the dialogue between Martha and Jesus as reported at Lararus' tomb. Jesus is immediately met upon arrival by Martha's cry, "If you had been here . . .," which, whatever note of reproach may be detected in it, is followed by her expression of confidence to Jesus that God will grant whatever he asks. When Jesus replies to her, "Your brother will rise again," her response as we are given it sounds traditionally creedal and formulaic: "I know that he will rise again in the resurrection on the last day" (Jn 11.23-24). Martha having made reference to "the last day," Jesus answers in the present tense: "I am the resurrection and the life," in whom those who believe though they die will live. He questions if Martha believes this. For a second time her reply sounds formulaic, creed-like, almost catechetical: "Yes, Lord, I believe that you are the Messiah, the Son of God, the one coming into the world" (Jn 11.25-27).

As they move closer to the gravesite, Martha gives voice to what she believes in a very different register, a blurting out, so it sounds, not at all scripted or formulaic. The change of tone is unmistakable. For, at the very moment that Jesus asks that the stone be rolled back, what we hear from Martha now confronting the remains of what is passing away is, "Lord, already there is a stench because he has been dead four days" (Jn 11.39). There is no sound this time of a rote recitation of creed or doctrine, no scripted catechesis, no distancing statements of belief about what she affirms will happen on "the last day," just to our ears a realistic acknowledgement of knowing what passing away entails, the stench of death in all its power to destroy the life we most closely relate to and most deeply love. Martha, in this statement, despite her grief, does not sound like someone who has lost her grip on reality. She rather sounds like someone who knows she is now facing the form of this world that is passing away. And, once again, as in her initial cry with which she greeted Jesus' arrival, we may detect a lingering note of reproach that this reality in her grip is not worth holding on to. As her mention again of four days implies, had Jesus come just four days earlier when she had summoned him in keeping with the time of Lazarus' passing away, things could — so we gather her point to be — have turned out quite differently. Death would have been denied the life of her brother, if Jesus had only kept to death's time.

What this news from Bethany makes plain is that whatever Martha's grip on reality at the tomb, it fails to grasp what is coming to pass. As John's account portrays the situation, an arrival of "the resurrection and the life" now at hand in the present tense as her Lord is standing right with her. She is not left alone. In this instance, death is being denied its power, not in terms of what is passing away but in terms of what is coming to pass. At the cry of Jesus, "Lazarus, come forth . . ." we hear of no "if only" regret based upon time that has passed away, no deferral of life until some "last day." The tense in John's account is present: "I *am* the resurrection and the life," says the Lord to whom Martha and Mary cry out. With this cry of Jesus, in contrast to theirs, death is said to be denied its bondage over life. What we hear is, "The dead man came out, his hands and feet bound with strips of cloth, and his face wrapped in a cloth. Jesus said to them, 'Unbind him, and let him go.'" (Jn 11.43-44).

We can, depending upon where we are coming from, and how much of death and loss we have faced, identify in varying degrees with the cry of Martha and Mary. Their words speak for us. Not so with this cry of Jesus and with what we hear happening with Lazarus coming forth from death. If this second cry speaks at all today, it speaks *to* us and not *for* us. That is to say, it is not a call we can make, any more than is the call of Martha and Mary to make Jesus' arrival conform to the time of Lazarus' passing away. Any identifying with what we hear in this second instance would seem not to be our identifying with this cry as if it were one coming from us, but rather somehow as our being identified by this cry as one coming to us. By juxtaposing the two cries at the same site of death in relating the news of what happens at Bethany, the Gospel accounts present their hearers with an incommensurability that purports at least to be of life and death proportions. The states of affairs as depicted are not univocal. What we hear is that the life summoned forth from death by the power of the resurrection does not come to pass in compliance with the summons issued in accordance with what is passing away. With the cry of Jesus the unprecedented takes precedence.

3. *The Bishop of Marseilles or a Hope of Life and Death Proportions?*

Given the graphic details of the narrated events leading up to the rais-ing of Lazarus, it is notable that with one exception we hear no news of his afterlife reported in the Gospels. The one exception is a brief mention of Lazarus later at table with Jesus and his sisters (Jn 12.2) — a reference suggestive of the table fellowship associated with the coming *basileia* of God in other Gospel accounts of Jesus' words at the Last Supper (Lk. 22.28-30) — with an added comment that the Chief Priests sought to kill him because the reports of his raising had led many to believe in Jesus (Jn 12.10-11). In this respect the witness of any afterlife by the power that the Gospel of John identifies in the present tense as at work in "the resurrection and the life" remains, as the testimony of Ephesians expresses it, "far more than all we can ask or imagine" (Eph. 3.20). This, it may be noted parenthetically, did not prevent a medieval folklore from imagining sightings of the family from Bethany later adrift without oars on the Mediterranean Sea and eventually coming ashore in southern France in time for Lazarus to be installed as the first Bishop of Marseilles, with relics of his remains rumored to be preserved there to this day![23]

In seeking to be attentive to all this, listening, as it were, in the posture of Mary, we may now ask: What hope realistically is there in all this? To be sure, this scene we hear of from Bethany can be dismissed as merely a biblical theme-park spectacle, a first-century tale restaged with adjustments for modern amplification. There are other stories of the dead being raised in the ancient world and literalistic accounts of the miraculous that only the most credulous seekers of signs would claim to base their hopes on today. Or, hearing this news from Bethany today may indeed convey a hope of life and death proportions.

For Christian faith the significance of all reports of death's overcoming derives from the witnessed power of Jesus Christ's own death on the cross and resurrection from the dead. This enacted passion shapes the church's liturgy, its preaching, its sacraments, and its service, and confronts its followers, along with Martha, on the way from rote to recognition. The news of what takes place at Bethany assumes this larger message, and provides a key instance of its import in bold relief. Faced by what is passing away, there is a fear of death and loss that the grief-stricken reports of the Gospel make no attempt to deny. Being faced by what is coming to pass, there is no fear of death, for the arrival on the scene is of a "perfect love that casts out all fear" (1 Jn 4.18). The promise to come is never witnessed as a deferral of grace. The "last day" is the day "at hand." The *there*, once again, is proclaimed to be *here* on the scene of greatest loss without ceasing to be *there* at the last when the last enemy is destroyed. "Do not let your hearts be troubled," are the words we hear of Jesus, "and do not let them be afraid" (Jn 14.27).

To return then to our most demanding question: What then is the hope of heaven, if any, expressed in these parameters? At the least this much we can acknowledge, to sum up from the foregoing observations: The "real world" is proclaimed to be one in which there is life currently arriving on the scene, in whatever situation we are facing, that is stronger than any undeniable loss threatening us, including death. I say "we" in a nonrestrictive sense, for this coming of life we hear of at the tomb of Lazarus is as unbounded in its embrace as the love it embodies, a love without exception, inbreaking at hand in the situation of each and all. This life is not conditional upon the state of affairs prior to its coming, nor is it subject to prior approximations. News of this life is expressed and reaches us, wherever we are coming from, in juxtapositions of incommensurability — which is to say, this news is not expressed, or recognized as such, literalistically, but parabolically — and it is only instantiated as real life apocalyptically by the taking place in the present tense where we are of an arrival upon the scene that is unprecedented.

Further, the life that we hear is called forth from death by the power identified in the present tense as "the resurrection and the life" is no abstract immortality of a disembodied soul above the stars and Milky Way, nameless and without a personal identity. In what we hear of the cry of Jesus to "come here with me," the precise name of the one whom he is said to love is spoken, "Lazarus, come forth!" This same personal note is sounded in other testimonies of the Gospel as well. In such words of Jesus as, "I go to prepare a place for you," and "will come again and will take you to myself," the "you" addressed in this context is personal, not impersonal, and plural, not singular or solitary (Jn 14.2-3).[24] In the face of all that undeniably causes us most to fear, including death, the actual arrival on the scene of the life that proves stronger than death is never too late. Given eyes to see and ears to hear what happens at Bethany, this may sound like the best news one could ever hear.

In these notes again we hear the contrapuntal variations of the leitmotif we have been attempting to follow in listening to the Gospel news of an incalculable forthcoming of heaven at hand. That this news of life unprecedented taking precedence is said to lack the credentials of credibility for a trustworthy hope is a further point of this extraordinary saga that the Gospel testimony makes no attempt to cover up. In fact, we hear the charge of false credentials of credibility raised specifically with reference to the coming of heaven.

The Genealogy of Heaven: "Whose Father and Mother We Know"

In the reports of what happens at Bethany no explicit mention is made of heaven, though the news of a coming upon the scene of "the resurrection and the life" in the present tense is definitely on message with what we hear in other Gospel testimonies that do speak of heaven. The explicit references come earlier in John's Gospel, and once again the present tense in the reported words of Jesus is said to provoke a reaction. This time the objection is not over his delayed arrival but over genealogy. The complaint, so we hear in this instance, is prompted by Jesus' words, "I am the bread that came down from heaven" (Jn 6.41). Those raising the complaint are quoted as objecting, "Is not this Jesus, the son of Joseph, whose father and mother we know? How can he now say, 'I have come down from heaven'" (Jn 6.42)?

Transposed into yet another key, we may hear a reprise of these objectors' questions in Johannes Weiss's description of a modern world-view, secure in its confidence of knowing what is enduring, a worldview in which, as he writes, "we do not await a Kingdom of God which is to come down from heaven."[25] Weiss thought this modern lack of expectation regarding heaven's coming represented the decisive difference from the attitude of the original hearers of Jesus' message — from that of "primitive Christianity" as he termed it — but that assumption is not borne out by what we hear of those questioning Jesus' heavenly credentials in this report from the Fourth Gospel. Even adjusting our modern earplugs, it is hard to believe that Weiss actually concludes by saying, ". . . We will at least approximate Jesus' attitude in a different sense, if we make the basis of our life the precept . . . 'Live as if you were dying.'"[26] That what is coming from heaven to earth cannot be approximated in such terms by what is passing away on earth is apparently news that both the original objectors to Jesus and Weiss's modern counterparts equally miss. What they share is expressed in words we have noted by which Jesus reportedly characterized his final entry into Jerusalem: "You did not recognize the time of your visitation" (Lk. 19.44). The direction Weiss advocates is exactly the reverse of what we hear in Paul's exclamation to his beloved Corinthians: "We are treated as . . . dying, and see — we are alive" (2 Cor. 6.8-9).

The implied assumption of Jesus' questioners is apparently that what is creditable is what counts as legitimate genetically. We hear the same credentials of legitimacy questioned genetically even before Jesus is born in the nativity account of Matthew. Joseph, described as a "righteous man," and thereby fearing the exposure of "public disgrace" in his association with Mary, resolves, so we hear, to divorce himself from the life that the Holy Spirit is conceiving to bring into the world in Mary's child. So great is this fear of moral illegitimacy that it takes an angel to appear to him in a dream with the words, "Joseph, . . . do not be afraid" (Mt. 1.20).

The question of genealogy figures prominently in the introduction of the Gospel of Matthew, which begins with the words, "An account of the genealogy (γενέσεως) of Jesus Christ the son of David, the son of Abraham" (Mt. 1.1). Older generations of Sunday school students raised on the King James Version of the Bible will be familiar with attempts to memorize these "begats." A favorite fifteenth-century carol of Jesus' birth equally familiar to us from celebrations of Christmas tells "of Jesse's lineage coming."[27] Philosophically, the term "genealogy," from Nietzsche to Foucault, has been used to denote reasoning disputing the legitimacy of assumptions about where claims to knowledge are coming from, reasoning which in turn has prompted further critiques of the genealogist's own self-awareness.[28] In both the scriptural objectors' questioning of how Jesus' claim to be present among them as one coming from heaven can be credited, assuming "his father and mother we know," and a modern project of philosophical genealogy that disputes certifications of knowledge claims based upon assumptions of the filial relation or family resemblance of ideas, what is at stake is how incommensurate identifications of a subject challenge the legitimacy of knowledge claims based upon precedence.

The genealogy we hear at the beginning of the Gospel of Matthew testifies to Jesus' descent from Abraham. The complaint we hear raised in the Gospel of John is said to be provoked because Jesus claims descent from heaven. These two descents, the earthly genealogy from Abraham leading up to the Joseph and Mary whom the questioners say they know, and the heavenly descent not identifiable in terms of filial precedence, but rather described by Jesus' words we hear in John's Gospel as "living bread" given for the life of the world as "my flesh," are juxtapositions of testimony regarding Jesus as the life of the world not reducible to a common generic denominator. This is a different issue from what later becomes known in church doctrine as the two natures of Christ, human and divine. Rather, it is that the questioners as we hear of them cannot grasp what is coming by means of their grasp of the past.

The difference may be illustrated by two contrasting terms in the Greek of the New Testament that, taken in context, are used in referring to incommensurate ways of claiming to know where Jesus is coming from: *kata sarka* ("according to the flesh") and *en sarki* ("in the flesh"). The first usage is found in Paul's statement that even though we once regarded Christ "*kata sarka*" we regard him in this way no longer (2 Cor. 5.16). As previously noted, an English translation that perhaps best conveys the contextual meaning of *kata sarka* in this instance is "according to our familiar way of judging appearances." Contrasted with this way of regarding Jesus is the call to test the spirits to see whether they are from God that we hear in 1 John 4.2. "By this you know the Spirit of God: every spirit that confesses that Jesus Christ has come *en sarki* is from God." Such a confession involves more than a mere assertion that Jesus once lived in the past. The New Testament scholar Martinus C. de Boer writes, "The use of the term 'flesh' in 1 John 4.2 . . . figuratively emphasizes the *concreteness* or *tangibility* of Jesus Christ's effective saving action, of his 'coming' . . . Discipleship is to be just as concrete or tangible."[29] A recognition of this scriptural contrast between regarding Christ "in the flesh" of his coming from heaven as the life-bread of the world, or regarding Christ merely "according to the flesh" of outward appearances subject to passing away, is expressed in the Latin of Martin Luther's assertion that Christ is known *in carne*, but not *secundum carnem*.[30]

What may sound newsworthy even to those familiar with these reports is that it is the descent from heaven that is said to identify the real life *en sarki* in the present. It is this life in the flesh and blood reality of the present that those questioning Jesus' credentials are portrayed as missing. So sure are they that they know where real life comes from by knowing what has gone before that they, just as Martha and Mary at the tomb of Lazarus, fail to recognize what is happening in the present. In short, their questions show that they are missing the one real hope of the present time that, according to the news of the Gospel, is exactly the difference heaven makes. It is this hope of heaven in Christ's coming that, in listening to the Gospel, we hear described by one word more than any other, "the hope of *glory*" (Col. 1.27).

On Hand "This Day" for "The Glory, Forever"

That the difference heaven makes in the face of all present opposition is the creating of an apocalypse of glory is a message conveyed in Paul's words, "I consider that the sufferings of this present time are not worth comparing with the glory about to be *apocalypsed* to us" (Rom. 8.18).

Similarly, he writes that while we groan under burdens in "the earthly tent we live in," our confident longing is "to be clothed with our heavenly dwelling," a "building from God, a house not made with hands" (2 Cor. 5.1-4). The verb "apocalypsed," as has been noted, is perhaps best understood in this context to mean *revealed as real, not by what is in place and passing away, but by what is taking place and newly coming to pass.* And what is this glory that at once calls attention to the sufferings of the present time, and yet is said to be incomparable in surpassing them — what kind of dwelling in heaven, which calls for reference not to the sky but to the groaning of earth's burdens in being described for earthly hearers as a house not made with hands? And most of all, whose "present time" is this day of which we hear for whom the news of such heavenly glory forever is intended?[31]

From a perspective directed toward "how we succeed" in the task of practicing moral virtue, one commentator has written, "The saints teach us that in the eventide of life we shall be judged on our loves."[32] We may be judged on our loves, but the glory for which we hear Jesus pray looking toward heaven in the Gospel of John points in a different direction, a direction not focused on the virtue of our loves but on our being loved: "The glory that you have given me I have given them . . . *that the world may know that . . . you . . . have loved them even as you have loved me*" (Jn 17.22-23). It is only from this direction that we hear Lazarus identified: "Lord, he whom you love is ill" (Jn 11.3); "See how he loved him!"(Jn 11.35). And as to the "them" to whom these words of glory apply, this we also hear: "I do not pray for these only," as the Fourth Gospel reports Jesus' reference to his disciples, "but also for those who believe in me through their word." (Jn 17.20). It is, so we hear, the news of this "also" that indicates no restriction upon whose "present time" it is where the *basileia* of heaven is at hand, or for whom the glory of being loved this day beyond every power of death is to be apocalypsed. It is this "also" to whom heaven is forthcoming, referring to all for whom we hear that Jesus prays in a love so unrestricted, in Paul's words, that from it nothing in life or death "can separate us" (Rom. 8.38-39).

In every "this day" situation of life and death we face a passing away and a coming to pass, a *basileia* or state of affairs arriving unprecedented on the scene as at Bethany, not according to our stipulations but better, with life from heaven that is stronger than all death's opposition to it. The call we hear is to seek this *basileia* in the promise of the reported words of Jesus not to be afraid, "for it is your Father's good pleasure to give you the *basileia*" (Lk. 12.32). "Where I am, there you may be also" are the words of promise we hear (Jn 14.3). In sum, we are called to be *on* hand for that which is *at* hand, but not *in* hand, an unprecedented glory of not being left orphaned but of being loved in a community of new creation beyond all that we can ask or imagine.

The scriptures cited throughout these pages are not meant as proof texts but as notes scoring a hearing of what Emily Dickinson called "the species beyond" this world's inconclusiveness that is "invisible as music but positive as sound." According to the notes of this hearing, a Sabbath is being prepared for us where a healing of our own withered hands, unable to grasp the glory of heaven's reality, signals the one thing coming that makes all the difference in the world.

NOTES

— ❖ —

Chapter 1: Hearing of Heaven Today

1. Rudolf Bultmann, "New Testament and Mythology," 1941, *Kerygma and Myth*, edited by Hans Werner Bartsch (SPCK, 1960), p. 4. I have altered the translation, which reads "traditional sense," to conform more exactly to the German original *"alten Sinne."* German: *". . . (D)en 'Himmel' im alten Sinne gibt es für uns gar nicht mehr."* *Kerygma Und Mythos*, (Hamburg: Reich & Heidrich — Evangelisher Verlag, 1948), p. 18.

2. Stuart Leggatt, ed., *Aristotle: On the Heavens (ΠΕΡΙ ΟΥΡΑΝΟΥ, De Caelo) I & II* (Warminster, Wiltshire: Aris & Phillips, 1995), 278b11, pp. 88–89.

3. Ibid., 270b20, pp. 58–59.

4. Augustine, *Confessions*, XII, 9. Since "the highest heaven" is still part of creation, even though the highest and thus, in Augustine's designation, an "intellectual" rather than a material creation, he distinguishes its participation in eternity (*particeps aeternitatis*) from God's own eternal triunity.

5. Dante Alighieri, *The Divine Comedy: Paradiso*, XXXIII, 145.

6. J. Edward Wright, *The Early History of Heaven* (New York: Oxford University Press, 2000).

7. Colleen McDannell & Bernhard Lang, *Heaven: A History* (New Haven: Yale University Press, 1988).

8. Carol Zaleski and Philip Zaleski, eds., *The Book of Heaven: An Anthology of Writings from Ancient to Modern Times* (New York: Oxford University Press, 2000).

9. Jeffrey Burton Russell, *A History of Heaven: The Singing Silence* (Princeton: Princeton University Press, 1997). See also Alister E. McGrath, *A Brief History of Heaven* (Oxford, UK: Blackwell, 2003), for imagery of "the human longing to *see* God" drawn explicitly from a theologically informed range of Christian literary sources.

10. See Christopher Morse, *Not Every Spirit: A Dogmatics of Christian Disbelief* (New York: T.&T. Clark/Continuum, 2nd edn, 2009).

11. David Van Biema, "Does Heaven Exist?," *Time*, March 24, 1997, pp. 70–78. See also, *Newsweek*, August 12, 2002, featuring a cover article by Lisa Miller on the variety of depicted visions of an after-death heaven, describing "the contemporary, mainstream view" of heaven as "whatever you dream it is," pp. 44–51.

12. For the Apostle's Creed in Latin and English, see Jaroslav Pelikan and Valerie Hotchkiss (eds), *Creeds and Confessions of Faith in the Christian Tradition* (Vol. 1, New Haven and London: Yale University Press, 2003), p. 669.

13. While it is the case that heaven itself is said to "pass away" (Ps. 102.25-28), be "changed" like God's "clothing" along with earth before the Word of God that endures forever, the promise is given of a "new heaven" and earth coming to pass (Mt. 24.35; 2 Pet. 3.12-13; Rev. 21.1-2; see also Isa. 34.4, 57.6, 65.17, 66.22). The contrast between the new heaven of God's new creation that is coming to pass, and the former heaven of God's creation that is passing away, remains.

14. John Calvin, *Institutes of the Christian Religion*, 1559, III, 21, 1; IV, 1, 9.

15. Strikingly, it is precisely the steadfast love (*hesed*) of the Lord, said to be "never ceasing," that is equally described in Lam. 3.22-23 as "new every morning." Similarly, the words of the prophet Isaiah are, "See, the former things have come to pass, and new things I now declare; before they spring forth, I tell you of them. Sing to the Lord a new song . . ." (Isa. 42.9-10). This call to "sing to the Lord a new song" finds repeated expression in the Psalms (cf. Ps. 33.3, 40.3, 96.1, 98.1, 144.9, and 149.1).

16. Emily Dickinson, "This World is not Conclusion," written c. 1862, first published 1896, *The Complete Poems of Emily Dickinson*, edited by Thomas H. Johnson (Little, Brown and Company, 1955), #501, p. 243.

17. See also 2 Chronicles 2.6 and 6.18.

18. "Crown Him with Many Crowns," words by Matthew Bridges, 1851, and Godfrey Thring, 1874. Allusion is made to Revelation 19.11, 13: "Then I saw heaven opened, and . . . [One] . . . clothed in a robe dipped in blood, and his name is called The Word of God."

19. Dietrich Bonhoeffer, *The Cost of Discipleship* (New York: The Macmillan Company, 1937, 1963), pp. 45–60.

20. The point is still illustrated by the NRSV translation: "In the beginning when God created the heavens and the earth . . ." (Gen. 1.1).

21. *Rufinus: A Commentary on the Apostles' Creed*, trans. with commentary by J.N.D. Kelly (Newman Press, 1955), pp. 36–37.

22. Saint Augustine, *Confessions* (Oxford, 1991), trans. with notes by Henry Chadwick, xiii, 16, p. 253. Chadwick documents the influence upon Augustine's thinking here of Plotinus and Porphyry, pp. 249–259.

23. *Ibid.*, xxiv, 33, p. 264.

24. *Ibid.*, xxxii, 43, p. 271.

25. See J. Louis Martyn, *Galatians, The Anchor Bible Vol. 33A* (New York: Doubleday, 1997), pp. 441–443, 462–466.

26. *The Epistle to Diognetus*, Ch. 5, vs. 4, 8-9, *The Apostolic Fathers II*

(The Loeb Classical Library, Cambridge: Harvard University Press, 1950), pp. 358–361.

27. Karl Barth, *Church Dogmatics*, III, 1, *The Doctrine of Creation* (Edinburgh: T. & T. Clark, 1958, # 51, "The Ambassadors of God and their Opponents," pp. 369–531. See reference to "the *entourage* accompanying God" on p. 486.

28. This is a point to which Immanuel Kant ascribed critical moral significance in *Religion within the Limits of Reason Alone*, 1793, 2nd edn 1794 (New York: Harper Torchbooks Ed. 1960), p. 53, asterisk.

29. Aileen Kelly, "On Isaiah Berlin (1909–1997)," with Michael Ignatieff, Stuart Hampshire, and Alfred Brendel, *The New York Review of Books*, December 18, 1997, p. 12.

30. Adolf Harnack, *What Is Christianity?*, 1900 (New York: Harper & Brothers, 1957), p. 56.

31. See references in Mt. 13, 18.23, 20.1, and 22.2 ff.

Chapter 2: The Theology of Heaven

1. "Alleluia, Sing to Jesus," words by Samuel S. Wesley, 1868.

2. See, for example, Karl Barth's comments, *Church Dogmatics*, II, 1, *The Doctrine of God* (Edinburgh: T. & T. Clark, 1957), pp. 636–638.

3. Immanuel Kant, *Religion Within the Limits of Reason Alone*, 1793, 2nd edn 1794 (New York: Harper Torchbooks Ed., 1960), p. 91.

4. For the few uses of terms translated in the New Testament as "religion" or "religious," see *deisidaimonia* in Acts 17.22-23 and 25.19; *threskeia* in Acts 26.5, Colossians 2.18, and James 1.27; and *eusebeia* which is used positively in 1 Timothy 2.2, 4.78, and 3.16. A rejection of generic labeling finds expression in Christian theology in the acknowledgment of the Deuteronomic confession that besides the Lord God "there is no other" (Deut. 4.35), expressed in the axiom *Deus non est in genere* (cf. Thomas Aquinas, *Summa Theologiae* 1a.3, 5).

5. Alfred North Whitehead, *Religion in the Making* (Meridian Books, 1926, 1960), p. 16.

6. William James, *The Varieties of Religious Experience* (The Modern Library, 1902, 1936), pp. 31–32.

7. Johannes Weiss, *Jesus' Proclamation of The Kingdom of God* 1892 (Fortress, 1971), p. 133.

8. Johannes Weiss, JPKG, p. 135. The influential texts in this regard were Immanuel Kant's *Religion within the Limits of Reason Alone* (1793–94) and Albrecht Ritschl's three-volume, *The Christian Doctrine of Justification and Reconciliation* (1870–1874).

9. Johannes Weiss, JPKG, p. 135. I have corrected the English translation here that reads "counterpart" to reflect more accurately the oppositional sense of *verneinend* [as "countering"] in the German original, *Die Predigt Jesu vom Reiche Gottes* (Göttingen, 1892), p. 66.

10. Albert Schweitzer, *The Kingdom of God and Primitive Christianity*, 1950–51 (Seabury, 1968), p. 183.

11. Johannes Weiss, JPKG, p. 135.

12. Albert Schweitzer, KGPC, p. 115.

13. Cf. Rudolf Bultmann, *Jesus Christ and Mythology* (Charles Scribner's Sons, 1958), pp. 11–13, and "Autobiographical Reflections" (1956) in *Existence and Faith: Shorter Writings of Rufolf Bultmann*, ed. Schubert M. Ogden (Meridian Books, 1960), pp. 283–288.

14. Frans Overbeck, *Christentum und Kultur: Gedanken und Anmerkungen zur modern Theologie* (Basel: Benno Schwabe, 1919), p. 289. "Denn um etwas Anderes wäre es mir nicht zu tun als um den Nachweis des *finis Christianismi* am modernen Christentum." Referred to by Ulrich H. J. Körtner, *The End of the World: A Theological Interpretation* (Westminster/John Knox, 1995, German 1988), p. 9. See Franz Overbeck, *How Christian is Our Present-Day Theology?*, trans. by Martin Henry (T.& T. Clark/ Continuum, 2005).

15. Franz Overbeck, CUK, pp. 9–10. "Weder Christus für sich noch der Glaube, den er gefunden hat, haben wenigstens unter dem Namen Christentum historisches Dasein gehabt." Quoted by Karl Barth in *Theology and Church: Shorter Writings 1920–1928* (Harper & Row, 1962), p. 61.

16. Karl Barth, "Unsettled Questions for Theology Today" (1920) in *Theology and Church: Shorter Writings 1920–1928* (New York, NY: Harper & Row, 1962), pp. 57–58: "Some of us are not wholly surprised by Overbeck's revelations. We rejoice at this book. We greet it gladly in the hope that it will raise up comrades for us in our loneliness."

17. Johannes Weiss, JPKG, pp. 135–136.

18. Johannes Weiss, JPKG, pp. 135–136. The prayer Weiss quotes comes from *The Didache* 10.6, a handbook of church instruction attributed to the twelve apostles, c. 2nd century AD.

19. For reference to the millions of copies in print of *Left Behind* by Tim LaHaye and Jerry B. Jenkins (Wheaton, Ill.: Tyndale House, 1995), and the influence of their ensuing series, see Gershom Gorenberg, *The End of Days: Fundamentalism and the Struggle for the Temple Mount* (Oxford: Oxford University Press, 2000), pp. 30–54.

20. See parallels in *Matthew* 24.4-36, *Mark* 13.5-37, and *Luke* 21.8-36. Apocalyptic motifs are prominent in other New Testament writings as well, with Paul's reference in *1 Thessalonians* 5.17 to those who are alive at Christ's descent from heaven being "caught up in the clouds . . . to meet the Lord in the air" receiving special emphasis among biblical literalists as "the rapture."

21. Cf. George M. Marsden, *Fundamentalism and American Culture: The Shaping of Twentieth-Century Evangelicalism 1870–1925* (Oxford University Press, 1980). Foremost purveyor of Darby's dispensationalism in American evangelical circles was C. I. Scofield's widely circulated *Rightly Dividing the Word of Truth* (Fleming H. Revell, 1909).

22. Gershom Gorenberg, *The End Of Days: Fundamentalism and the Struggle for the Temple Mount* (Oxford: Oxford University Press, 2000), p. 55. Hal Lindsey's *The Late Great Planet Earth* was first published with C. C. Carlson by Zondervan Publishing House in 1970.

23. Origen (c. 185–c. 254), *On First Principles*, Bk. 4.

24. For a brief account, see Wilhelm Pauck's introduction to the medieval background of Martin Luther's exegesis, *Luther: Lectures on Romans, The Library of Christian Classics, Vol. XV* (Philadelphia: The Westminster Press, 1961), pp. xxvii–xxviii.

25. Hal Lindsey, *The Late Great Planet Earth*, with C. C. Carlson (Zondervan Publishing House, 1970), pp. 10 and 165.

26. *The Literalist*, Vols. 1–5 (Philadelphia: Orrin Rogers Publisher, 1840–1841).

27. The conservative Princeton theologian Charles Hodge thus defined "the plain historical sense" of the words of scripture as "the sense attached to them in the age and by the people to whom they were addressed," but criticized the premillennialist writers of *The Literalist* for assuming that this "plain sense" was necessarily the same as a univocally "literal sense." Charles Hodge, *Systematic Theology*, In Three Volumes, 1871–1873 (Wm. B. Eerdmans Publishing Company, 1986), Vol. 1, p. 187, and Vol. 3, pp. 865–868.

28. Thomas Aquinas, *Summa Theologiae*, 1A. 13, 15.

29. Thomas Aquinas, *Summa Theologiae*, 1A. 1, 10.

30. Cf. Jürgen Moltmann, *Theology of Hope* (Harper & Row, 1967), pp. 242–243, 270.

31. See especially Hans W. Frei, "The 'Literal Reading' of Biblical Narrative in the Christian Tradition: Does it Stretch or Will it Break?," *The Bible and the Narrative Tradition*, ed. Frank McConnell (New York: Oxford University Press, 1986), pp. 36–77.

32. Cf. Antonin Scalia, *A Matter of Interpretation: Federal Courts and the Law*, with commentary by Amy Gutmann, ed., Gordon S. Wood, Laurence H. Tribe, Mary Ann Glendon, and Ronald Dworkin (Princeton University Press, 1997).

33. Ernst Troeltsch, "Historical and Dogmatic Method in Theology," 1898, *Religion in History* (Fortress Press, 1991), p. 17.

34. Hal Lindsey, *The Late Great Planet Earth*, with C. C. Carlson (Zondervan Publishing House, 1970), p. 164.

35. Antecedents to this discussion of myth in the modern period date back to David Friedrich Strauss (1808–1874), of whom Albert Schweitzer writes that "prior to him the conception of myth was neither truly grasped nor consistently applied." Albert Schweitzer, *The Quest of the Historical Jesus* (New York: The Macmillan Company, 1959), p. 78. For a history of the term's modern usage see Gary Dorrien, *The Word as True Myth: Interpreting Modern Theology* (Louisville: Westminster John Knox Press, 1997).

36. Aristotle, *Metaphysics*, Bk. B 1000a 9, Bk. E 1026a 10–20, and Bk. K 1064b 3.

37. Rudolf Bultmann, *Kerygma and Myth*, ed. by Hans Werner Bartsch (SPCK, 1960), p. 3.

38. Rudolf Bultmann, *Jesus Christ and Mythology* (Charles Scribner's Sons, 1958), p. 40.

39. Rudolf Bultmann, *Kerygma and Myth*, ed. by Hans Werner Bartsch (SPCK, 1960), p. 10.

40. Rudolf Bultmann, *Jesus Christ and Mythology* (Charles Scribner's. Sons, 1958), pp. 68–70.

41. Rudolf Bultmann, *Jesus Christ and Mythology* (Charles Scribner's Sons, 1958), p. 18.

42. Rudolf Bultmann, "A Reply to the Theses of J. Schniewind," *Kerygma and Myth*, ed. by Hans Werner Bartsch, (SPCK, 1960), pp. 102–103. In the German original, *Kerygma Und Mythos* (Hamburg: Reich & Heidrich — Evangelisher Verlag, 1948), p. 135, Schniewind's question, *ob wir dem Mythos je entgehen können*, as cited by Bultmann, is answered by saying *nicht nur entbehren können, sondern auch entbehren müssen*. Both the German verbs *entgehen* and *entbehren* have been translated in the English version without distinction as "dispense with." For a later expression of his view, see Bultmann's *Jesus Christ and Mythology* (Charles Scribner's Sons, 1958), p. 68, where he seems to be responding directly to Tillich without mentioning him by name in writing that "to speak of God as acting does not necessarily mean to speak in symbols or images" in any manner to be understood as "mythological speech." Note also in this connection Bultmann's exchange of open letters with the philosopher Karl Jaspers in *Myth and Christianity: an Inquiry into the Possiblity of Religion without Myth* by Karl Jaspers and Rudolf Bultmann (The Noonday Press, 1958).

43. Paul Tillich, *Dynamics of Faith* (Harper & Brothers, 1957), p. 41.

44. Paul Tillich, *Systematic Theology*, Vol. 2 (University of Chicago Press, 1957), p. 152.

45. For the best analysis of Bultmann and late twentieth century criticisms see James F. Kay, *Christus Praesens: A Reconsideration of Rudolf Bultmann's Christology* (Grand Rapids: William B. Eerdmans Publishing Company, 1994).

46. Rudolf Bultmann, *Jesus Christ and Mythology* (Charles Scribner's Sons, 1958), pp. 69–70.

47. Paul Tillich, *Systematic Theology*, Vol.1 (University of Chicago Press, 1951), p. 277.

48. Paul Tillich, *Systematic Theology*, Vol. 3 (University of Chicago Press, 1963), pp. 418–419.

49. Paul Tillich, *Systematic Theology*, Vol. 3 (University of Chicago Press, 1963), pp. 360–361.

50. Paul Tillich, *Systematic Theology*, Vol. 3 (University of Chicago Press, 1963), p. 356. This complements his description of heaven elsewhere in his *Systematic Theology* where he writes of it in terms of qualities (Vol. 1, p. 277) and states of blessedness (Vol. 3, p. 418).

51. For Bultmann's own attention to this question and his view of Martin Heidegger's existentialist philosophy, see his 1956 "Autobiographical Reflections," and 1957 article, "Is Exegesis Without Presuppositions Possible?," in *Existence and Faith: Shorter Writings of Rudolf Bultmann*, ed. Schubert M. Ogden (New York: Meridian Books, Inc., 1960), pp. 283–296. Earlier, in 1941, he defended himself against the charge of imposing Heidegger's categories upon the New Testament by arguing that "the philosophers are saying the same thing as the New Testament and saying it quite independently." *Kerygma and Myth*, ed. Hans Werner Bartsch, (SPCK, 1960), p. 25.

52. Karl Barth, *Church Dogmatics*, III, 1, *The Doctrine of Creation* (Edinburgh: T. & T. Clark, 1958), p. 84. See *KD*, III, 1, p. 91.

53. Karl Barth, *Church Dogmatics*, III, 1, *The Doctrine of Creation* (Edinburgh: T. & T. Clark, 1958), p. 11; and *Church Dogmatics*, III, 3, *The Doctrine of Creation* (Edinburgh: T. & T. Clark, 1960), p. 374.

54. Karl Barth, *Church Dogmatics*, III, 1, *The Doctrine of Creation* (Edinburgh: T. & T. Clark, 1958), p. 84. Whether Barth and Bultmann ever accurately heard what each other was saying about the role of myth in relation to the news of heaven remained a disputed subject of their continual correspondence for over forty years. Barth finally concluded, despite Bultmann's repeated entreaties, that they were best likened to a whale and an elephant unable to communicate with each other in their own terms! See *Karl Barth — Rudolf Bultmann: Letters, 1922–1966*, ed. Bernd Jaspert (Grand Rapids: William B. Eerdmans Publishing Company, 1981), p. 105. In a later televised interview for *Viewpoint*, Barth also used the same analogy of the whale and the elephant to describe the failure to come to agreement between Emil Brunner and himself.

55. Karl Barth, *Church Dogmatics*, III, 1, *The Doctrine of Creation* (Edinburgh: T. & T. Clark, 1958), pp. 80–81.

56. Karl Barth, *Church Dogmatics*, III, 3, *The Doctrine of Creation* (Edinburgh: T. & T. Clark, 1960), p. 375. See *KD*, III, 3, p. 433.

57. Karl Barth, *Church Dogmatics*, III, 1, *The Doctrine of Creation* (Edinburgh: T. & T. Clark, 1958), p. 81. Barth's words here are "*praehistorischen Geschichtswirklichkeit.*" See *KD*, III, 1, p. 88.

58. Karl Barth, *Church Dogmatics*, III, 3, *The Doctrine of Creation* (Edinburgh: T. & T. Clark, 1960), p. 376.

59. See Hans Frei, *The Eclipse of Biblical Narrative: A Study in Eighteenth and Nineteenth Century Hermeneutics* (New Haven: Yale University Press, 1974) and "The 'Literal Reading' of Biblical Narrative in the Christian Tradition: Does It Stretch or Will It Break?," in *The Bible And The Narrative Tradition*, ed. Frank McConnell (New York: Oxford University Press, 1986), pp. 36–77.

60. See Hans Frei, *The Identity of Jesus Christ: The Hermeneutical Bases of Dogmatic Theology* (Philadelphia: Fortress Press, 1975).

61. Karl Barth, *Church Dogmatics*, IV, 3, First Half, *The Doctrine of Reconciliation* (Edinburgh: T. & T. Clark, 1961), pp. 176 and 179. See *KD* IV, 3, First Half, pp. 201 and 205.

62. Hans Frei, *The Eclipse of Biblical Narrative: A Study in Eighteenth and Nineteenth Century Hermeneutics* (New Haven: Yale University Press, 1974), p. 280.

63. See Francesca Aran Murphy's critique in *God is Not a Story: Realism Revisited* (Oxford, 2007).

64. Jürgen Moltmann, *Theology of Hope: On the Ground and the Implications of a Christian Eschatology* (New York: Harper & Row, 1967) and "Theology as Eschatology," published in *The Future of Hope*, ed. Frederick Herzog (New York: Herder and Herder, 1970), pp. 1–50. See Christopher Morse, *The Logic of Promise in Moltmann's Theology* (Philadelphia: Fortress Press, 1979).

65. For a partial selection from the later writings, see Moltmann's most explicit treatment of heaven as created in his Gifford Lectures of 1984–1985,

God in Creation: A New Theology of Creation and the Spirit of God (San Francisco: Harper & Row, 1985), pp. 158–184; his most comprehensive overall summary in *The Coming of God: Christian Eschatology* (Minneapolis: Fortress Press, 1996); and his reflections looking back on his initial ideas regarding the logic of promise and the hermeneutics of hope in *Experiences in Theology: Ways and Forms of Christian Theology* (Minneapolis: Fortress Press, 2000), pp. 86–179.

66. Jürgen Moltmann, *Theology of Hope: On the Ground and the Implications of a Christian Eschatology* (New York: Harper & Row, 1967), p. 188.

67. Jürgen Moltmann, *Theology of Hope: On the Ground and the Implications of a Christian Eschatology* (New York: Harper & Row, 1967), pp. 189–190.

68. Philip Melanchthon, *Loci Communes* (1555), xi, in *Melanchthon on Christian Doctrine: Loci Communes 1555*, ed. Clyde L. Manschreck (New York: Oxford University Press, 1965), p. 158.

69. A contrasting threefold depiction to the one given of God in Revelation 1.4, "who was and is and is to come," is given of the "beast" in opposition to God in Revelation 17.8 with the words, "it was and is *not* and is to come." In both cases the apocalyptic reference is directed to a future and speaks of a coming, but in the case of the evil "beast" the coming is said to be only to "destruction."

70. I have discussed this initial reaction further in "God's Promise As Presence," Ch. 9 in *Love: The Foundation of Hope*, ed. Frederic B. Burnham, Charles S. McCoy, and M. Douglas Meeks (San Francisco: Harper & Row), 1988, pp. 143–157.

71. Quotes here from Moltmann come from "Theology as Eschatology," in *The Future of Hope: Theology as Eschatology*, ed. Frederick Herzog (New York: Herder and Herder, 1970), pp. 9–16 and 158.

72. The insightful phrase "memory of the future" is Gabriel Marcel's description of prophetic hope in *Homo Viator: Introduction to a Metaphysics of Hope* (Chicago: H. Regnery, 1951), p. 53.

73. Letter from Bultmann to Barth dated, Marburg, November 11–15, 1952, number 94 in *Karl Barth — Rudolf Bultmann Letters 1922–1966*, ed. Bernd Jaspert (Grand Rapids: William B. Eerdmans Publishing Company, 1981), p. 87.

Chapter 3: The Reality of Heaven

1. The conventional typecasting at this point tends to classify Bultmann as a proponent of a general ontology, such as that proposed by the extentialist philosophy of Martin Heidegger, with Barth as an anti-philosophical opponent, and to debate the merits and demerits of a so-labeled foundational ontology, or "ontotheology" as such. In contrast, my interest here is with the less prefabricated posing of the reality question suggested by Bultmann's own words in asking how the Gospel news of heaven may be said to relate to how we think and speak of reality "in our everyday lives."

2. Paul Tillich, *Systematic Theology*, Vol. 3 (Chicago: The University of Chicago Press, 1963), p. 357.

3. Karl Barth, *Church Dogmatics*, III, 3, *The Doctrine of Creation* (Edinburgh: T. & T. Clark, 1950), p. 369.

4. For just one such acknowledgement among others see Karl Barth, CD, III, 3, p. 443: "It is inaccessible and unknown, but it is a real context of being. In its own very different way it is just as real as the earth which is ontically and noetically our sphere." See also CD, III, 3, p. 437. I am only page counting here the more explicit discussions in CD, III, 1, pp. 1–144 and III, 3, pp. 236–531.

5. Whatever may have been the grounds in Barth's early writings for Dietrich Bonhoeffer's comradely charge of "revelational positivism," it cannot be said that Barth simply asserts his interpretative claims without providing an often extensive (some would say, exhaustive!) accounting. The question, as Bonhoeffer's own life and work came to bear witness, is *how* most faithfully to account for such "reality."

6. Karl Barth, *Church Dogmatics*, II, 1, *The Doctrine of God* (Edinburgh: T. & T. Clark, 1957), p. 637. The date of the original German edition in which this quote first appears is 1940.

7. See in this connection the philosopher Giorgio Agamben's objection to the application of either "parable" or "apocalyptic" to Paul's sense of "messianic time" in *The Time That Remains: A Commentary on the Letter to the Romans* (Stanford, CA.: Stanford University Press, 2005), pp. 42–43, 62–64. My use of the terms here in expressing what I take to be the hermeneutical import of the Gospel's news of heaven as *parabolic significance* does not subscribe to Agamben's view of "parable" as implying here a restriction of the kingdom to language, or of "apocalyptic" as referring only to the last day, but actually resonates more with his thesis that what is at stake for Paul as messianic event "is present *en tō nun kairō*, as the revocation of every worldly condition, released from itself to allow for its use" (p. 43).

8. J. Louis Martyn, "The Apocalyptic Gospel in Galatians," *Interpretation*, Vol. 54, July 2000, p. 255. Also see Martyn's *Galatians: A New Translation with Introduction and Commentary*, The Anchor Bible, Vol. 33A (Doubleday, 1997), and *Theological Issues in the Letters of Paul* (Abingdon, 1997).

9. See references in Mt. 13, 18.23, 20.1, and 22.2 ff.

10. Ernst Troeltsch, "Historical and Dogmatic Method in Theology," 1898, *Religion in History* (Fortress Press, 1991), pp. 11–32.

11. John Drury, *The Parables in the Gospels: History and Allegory* (New York: Crossroad, 1985), p. 42.

12. William R. Herzog II, *Parables as Subversive Speech: Jesus as Pedagogue of the Oppressed* (Louisville: Westminster/ John Knox Press, 1994), p. 15.

13. Stephen L. Wailes, *Medieval Allegories of Jesus' Parables* (Berkeley and Los Angeles: University of California Press, 1987), p. 9. Wailes notes Augustine's admonition in *On Christian Doctrine*, III.9, "to be very careful lest you take figurative expressions literally."

14. Arland J. Hultgren, *The Parables of Jesus: A Commentary* (Grand Rapids: William B. Eerdmans Publishing Company, 2000), p. 2.

15. John Drury, *The Parables*, p. 33.

16. John Drury, *The Parables*, p. 27.
17. Cf. William R. Herzog II, *Parables as Subversive Speech*.
18. Cf. J. Louis Martyn, "Epistemology at the Turn of the Ages," *Theological Issues in the Letters of Paul* (Nashville: Abingdon Press, 1997), pp. 89–110.
19. Bertrand Russell, *Why I Am Not a Christian* (New York: Simon and Schuster, 1957), p. 19.
20. Bertrand Russell, *Why I Am Not a Christian* (New York: Simon and Schuster, 1957), p. 23.
21. Karl Barth, CD, III, 3, pp. 374–375 and 521. See *KD* III, 3, pp. 432 and 611.
22. See Karl Barth, CD, III, 1, especially pp. 94–168; and CD, III, 3, especially pp. 236–531.
23. Karl Barth, CD, III, 1, pp. 83–84.
24. Karl Barth, CD, III, 3, p. 376.
25. Karl Barth, CD, III, 3, p. 374; CD, III, 1, p. 81.
26. Karl Barth, CD, III, 3, p. 434.
27. Karl Barth, CD, III, 1, p. 81 and III, 3, p. 374.
28. Karl Barth, CD, III, 3, p. 485.
29. Karl Barth, CD, III, 1, p. 100.
30. Karl Barth, CD, III, 1, pp. 3, 17–18.
31. Karl Barth, CD, III, 3, pp. 374–375. See *KD*, III, 3, p. 433.
32. Karl Barth, *Church Dogmatics*, I, 1, *The Doctrine of the Word of God*, 2nd ed. (Edinburgh: T. & T. Clark, 1975), p. 133.
33. Karl Barth, "The Strange New World within The Bible," 1916, *The Word of God and The Word of Man* (Harper, 1957), pp. 28–50.
34. Karl Barth, CD, III, 3, p. 237.
35. Karl Barth, CD, III, 3, p. 521. See *KD*, III, 3, p. 611.
36. F. D. E. Schleiermacher, *Hermeneutics: The Handwritten Manuscripts*, ed. Heinz Kimmerle, *Manuscript 5*, 1829 (Missoula, Montana: Scholars Press, 1977), pp. 175–214.
37. F. D. E. Schleiermacher, *Hermeneutics: The Handwritten Manuscripts*, p. 226.
38. F. D. E. Schleiermacher, *Hermeneutics: The Handwritten Manuscripts*, *Manuscript 5*, p. 194.
39. Karl Barth, CD, III, 3, p.485.
40. Karl Barth, CD, III, 3, p. 529.
41. For Barth's discussion of evil as *Das Nichtige* see CD, III, 3, # 50, pp.289–368; see *KD* pp. 327-425 and also Wolf Krötke, *Sin and Nothingness in the Theology of Karl Barth* (1970), translated by Philip G. Ziegler and Christina-Maria Bammel and republished with a new Foreword by the author in *Studies in Reformed Theology and History*, Vol. NS10 (Princeton Theological Seminary, 2005).
42. Karl Barth, CD, III, 3, p. 521; *KD*, III, 3, p.611.
43. Karl Barth, *Church Dogmatics*, IV, 3, First Half, (T. & T. Clark, 1963), p. 117; *KD*, IV. 3, First Half, p. 131.
44. *Webster's New World College Dictionary*, Fourth Edition, 2006.
45. See Jacob Taubes, *The Political Theology of Paul*, 1993 (Stanford, 2004); Alain Badiou, *Saint Paul: The Foundation of Universalism*, 1997

(Stanford, 2003); Slavoj Žižek, *The Fragile Absolute* (Verso, 2000); and Giorgio Agamben, *The Time That Remains: A Commentary on the Letter to the Romans*, 2000 (Stanford: 2005). In this connection note also Theodore W. Jennings, Jr., *Reading Derrida/Thinking Paul: On Justice* (Stanford: 2006).

46. See Christopher Morse, "The Resurrection as Myth and as Fable: The Difference after Thirty Years," *In Search of Humanity and Deity: A Celebration of John Macquarrie's Theology*, ed. Robert Morgan (SCM Press, 2006), pp. 254–263.

47. Here I draw upon my earlier article, "The Virtue of Heaven: From Calvin to Cyber-talk and Back," *Modern Theology*, 19.3, July 2003, pp. 317–328.

48. Benjamin Woolley, *Virtual Worlds: A Journey in Hype and Hyperreality* (Blackwell, 1992).

49. Benjamin Woolley, VW, p. 60.

50. Benjamin Woolley, VW, p. 37.

51. With reference to Calvin's emphasis upon the Holy Spirit's power as *virtus*, François Wendel writes, "It was in a sermon which Erasmus had attributed to St. John Chrysostom and had included in the edition of his works published at Basle in 1530, that Calvin found the idea that the Holy Spirit is the bond of our union with Christ." *Calvin: Origins and Development of His Religious Thought* (Baker Books, 1963, 1997), pp. 350–351. Also, in discussing Christ's ascended presence, in II, 16, 14 of his *Institutes*, Calvin quotes Augustine. John Calvin, *Institutes of the Christian Religion*, The Library of Christian Classics, Vols 20–21 (Westminster, 1960), p. 523.

52. See John Calvin, *Institutes of the Christian Religion*, The Library of Christian Classics, Vol. XXI, ed. John T. McNeill (Philadelphia: Westminster, 1960), Bk. 4, Ch. 17, Par. 10, pp. 1370–1371, where Calvin discusses how Christ, now ascended in heaven, by the immeasurable *virtus* of the Holy Spirit "truly presents and shows his body" (*quin vere praestet atque exhibeat*) in the Lord's Supper. The Latin original is cited from *Calvini Opera, Vol. 5*, the *Institutio Christianae Religionis 1559*, ed. Petrus Barth and Guilelmus Niesel (Munich: Chr. Kaiser, 1926), p. 352.

53. John Calvin, ICR, IV, 17, 17–19, pp. 1379–1382.

54. John Calvin, ICR, IV, 17, 10, p. 1370.

55. John Calvin, ICR, IV, 17, 11, p. 1372.

56. John Calvin, ICR, IV, 17, 10, p. 1370.

57. John Calvin, ICR, II, 9, 3, p. 426.

58. John Calvin, ICR, see footnote 27, p. 1370, by Ford Lewis Battles: "For his habitual assertion of the mysterious power (*virtus*) operating in the sacraments, Calvin's doctrine has been called 'virtualism'." See also Laurence Hull Stookey, *Eucharist: Christ's Feast with the Church* (Abingdon Press, 1993), pp. 55–56.

59. For works that address theological issues from the standpoints of cyberspace theory and electronic technology see Margaret Wertheim, *The Pearly Gates of Cyberspace: A History of Space from Dante to the Internet* (W. W. Norton, 1999) and James E. Huchingson, *Pandemonium Tremendum: Chaos and Mystery in the Life of God* (Pilgrim Press, 2001). I am indebted to Peter Heltzel for bringing these to my attention.

Chapter 4: The Ethics of Heaven

1. "Life's Railway to Heaven," by M. E. Abbey and Charlie D. Tillman, 1920, cited from *Devotional Hymns* (Hope Publishing Co., 1947), p. 117.

2. J. Louis Martyn, *Galatians: A New Translation with Introduction and Commentary*, The Anchor Bible, Vol. 33A (New York: Doubleday, 1997), p. 502. See also Martyn, *Theological Issues in the Letters of Paul* (Nashville: Abingdon Press, 1997), p. 233. Needless to say, my indebtedness to Martyn by no means presumes his agreement with me on all points, or pretends in these few remarks to convey the full range of his own thought. Martyn translates Gal. 5.13–24 as follows, p. 9.

> 13. For you were called to freedom, brothers and sisters; only do not allow freedom to be turned into a military base of operations for the Flesh, active as a cosmic power. On the contrary, through love be genuine servants of one another. 14. For the whole of the Law has been brought to completion in one sentence: "You shall love your neighbor as yourself!" 15. But if you snap at one another, each threatening to devour the other, take care that you are not eaten up by one another! 16. In contradistinction to the Teachers, I, Paul, say to you: Lead your daily life guided by the Spirit, and, in this way, you will not end up carrying out the Impulsive Desire of the Flesh. 17. For the Flesh is actively inclined against the Spirit, and the Spirit against the Flesh. Indeed these two powers constitute a pair of opposites at war with one another, the result being that you do not actually do the very things you wish to do. 18. If, however, in the daily life of your communities you are being consistently led by the Spirit, then you are not under the authority of the Law. 19. The effects of the Flesh are clear, and those effects are: fornication, vicious immorality, uncontrolled debauchery, 20. the worship of idols, belief in magic, instances of irreconcilable hatred, strife, resentment, outbursts of rage, mercenary ambition, dissensions, separation into divisive cliques, 21. grudging envy of the neighbor's success, bouts of drunkenness, nights of carousing, and other things of the same sort. In this regard, I warn you now, just as I warned you before: those who practice things of this sort will not inherit the Kingdom of God. 22. By contrast, the fruit borne by the Spirit is love, joy, peace, patience, kindness, generosity, faith, 23. gentleness, self-control. The Law does not forbid things of this kind! 24. And those who belong to Christ Jesus have crucified the Flesh, together with its passions and desires.

3. For an overview of the history of ethics since Socrates through the 1960s, see the entry by Raziel Abelson and Kai Nielsen in *The Encyclopedia of Philosophy*, Vol. 3 (Macmillan, 1967), pp. 81–117.

4. Aristotle, *Nicomachean Ethics* (Hackett Publishing Company, 1985), especially Chs 1–5, pp. 1–70. Re. virtues, "They are up to us and voluntary." Ch.5, section 3.46, p. 70. For Aristotle, the slavery of some, i.e. those considered to lack the ability for any virtue other than servitude to a master, is

NOTES TO PAGES 76–87 ❖ 135

held to be naturally necessary for the social good of all. See *Aristotle Politics: Books I and II* (Clarendon Press, 1995), I iii–I vi, pp. 4–9.

5. For Calvin's rejection of Aristotle's and "the philosophers'" attribution of virtue to our powers see his *Institutes of the Christian Religion*, The Library of Christian Classics, Vol. XX, Bk. 2, Ch. 2, Par. 3, pp. 257–258, and Bk. 2, pp. Ch. 5, Par. 2, pp. 318–319. That *virtus* historically came to take on anthropologically the connotation of virility, and thereby the privileging of masculinity, has rightly been exposed by feminist scholars. See Catherine Keller's study of "the *Wirkungsgeschichte* of the Apocalypse, that is . . . the history of its effects as a text on other texts" in regard to gender issues, *Apocalypse Now and Then: A Feminist Guide to the End of the World* (Beacon Press, 1996), p. 89.

6. Joseph Fletcher, *Situation Ethics: The New Morality* (The Westminster Press, 1966), pp. 30–31.

7. Joseph Fletcher, SE, p. 157.

8. Joseph Fletcher, SE, p. 31.

9. Immanuel Kant, *Religion within the Limits of Reason Alone*, 1763–94 (Harper & Row, 1960), p. 113.

10. Immanuel Kant, RWLRA, p. 180.

11. Johannes Weiss, *Jesus' Proclamation of the Kingdom of God* 1892 (Fortress, 1971), p. 136.

12. Johannes Weiss, JPKG, p. 135.

13. Johannes Weiss, JPKG, p. 135.

14. Johannes Weiss, JPKG, p. 62.

15. Paul Tillich, *Systematic Theology*, Vol. 1 (The University of Chicago Press, 1951), p. 277.

16. Karl Barth, *The Epistle to the Romans* (Oxford University Press, 1933), p. 432.

17. Karl Barth, *Church Dogmatics*, II, 1, *The Doctrine of God* (T. & T. Clark, 1957), p. 637.

18. See Karl Barth's 1928–29 *Ethics* (The Seabury Press, 1981) and *Church Dogmatics*, I, 2, *The Doctrine of the Word of God* (T. & T. Clark, 1956), "Dogmatics As Ethics," pp. 782–796; CD, II, 2, *The Doctrine of God* (T. & T. Clark, 1957), "The Command of God," pp. 509–781; CD, III, 4, *The Doctrine of Creation* (T. & T. Clark, 1961), "The Command of God the Creator," pp. 3–685; and CD, IV.4, Lecture Fragments, *The Christian Life* (T. & T. Clark, 1981). See also John Webster, *Barth's Moral Theology: Human Action in Barth's Thought* (Eerdmans, 1998).

19. Jürgen Moltmann, *Theology of Hope* (Harper & Row, 1967), p. 40.

20. Jürgen Moltmann, *The Coming of God: Christian Eschatology* (Fortress Press, 1996).

21. For these lectures, compiled from student notes, see Dietrich Bonhoeffer, *Wer ist und wer war Jesus Christus? Seine Geschichte und sein Geheimnis* (Furche-Verlag, 1962), p. 49, and the English translation, *Christ the Center* (Harper & Row, 1966, 1978), pp. 59–60, titled in England *Christology* (Collins, 1966).

22. Dietrich Bonhoeffer, *Ethics*, Dietrich Bonhoeffer Works, Vol. 6 (Fortress, 2005), p. 261.

23. Dietrich Bonhoeffer, *Ethics*, p. 372.
24. *No Rusty Swords: Letters, Lectures and Notes 1928–1936*, Edwin H. Robertson, ed. (New York: Harper and Row, 1965), p. 118. ["Die entscheidende Aufgabe ist heute das Gespräch zwischen dem Protestantismus ohne Reformation und den Kirchen der Reformation." *Gesammelte Schriften*, I (Munich: Chr. Kaiser Verlag, 1958), p. 354.]
25. Dietrich Bonhoeffer, *The Communion of Saints: A Dogmatic Inquiry into the Sociology of the Church*, 1927 (New York: Harper & Row, 1963), and *Act and Being*, 1931 (New York: Harper & Row, 1961).
26. *The Communion of Saints*, p. 20.
27. *NRS*, p. 89. [*GS*, I, p. 87.]
28. *NRS*, p. 89–90. [*GS*, I, p. 88.]
29. *NRS*, p. 90. [*GS*, I, pp. 88–89.]
30. *NRS*, pp. 99. [*GS*, I, p. 331.]
31. *NRS*, p. 117. [*GS*, I, p. 354.]
32. *NRS*, p. 104. [*GS*, I, p. 337.]
33. *NRS*, p. 184. [*GS*, I, pp. 163–164.]
34. *NRS*, p. 112–114. [*GS*, I, p. 347–349.] See especially in this regard Josiah Ulysses Young III, *No Difference in the Fare: Dietrich Bonhoeffer and the Problem of Racism* (Eerdmans, 1998).
35. *NRS*, p. 114. [*GS*, I, p. 350.]
36. The Greek words with forms usually translated "religion" or "religious" in English versions of the New Testament are *threskeia*, "reverencing"(cf. Acts 26.5, Colossians 2.18, and James 1.27); *deisidaimonia*, "treating as gods" (cf. Acts 17.22–23 and 25.19); and *eusebeia*, which is used positively in 1 Timothy 2.2, 4.7–8, and 3.16.
37. Immanuel Kant, *Religion within the Limits of Reason Alone*, 1793–1794 (Harper Torchbook, 1960), p. 125.
38. John Calvin, ICR, Vol. XX, I, 4, pp. 47–51; II, 6, 4, pp. 346–347; II, 16, 3, pp. 505–506.
39. Martin Luther, *The Heidelberg Disputation* (1518), The Library of Christian Classics, Vol. XVI, *Luther: Early Theological Works* (Westminster, 1962), # XXI, pp. 291–292.
40. For Bonhoeffer's characteristic use of the term *Menschwerdung* rather than *Inkarnation*, see Clifford Green, "Editor's Introduction to the English Edition," *Dietrich Bonhoeffer: Ethics, Dietrich Bonhoeffer Works*, Vol. 6 (Fortress Press, 2005), p. 6.
41. *Letters and Papers from Prison*, entry dated May 5, 1944, (Macmillan, 1972; Simon & Schuster, enlarged edn, 1997), pp. 168–169.
42. Karl Barth, *Church Dogmatics*, IV, 3, # 69, p. 91.
43. For a critique of the idea that Barth's later, more nuanced position with regard to religion in CD, I, 2, # 17 is identical to Bonhoeffer's, see the newer translation of this section with an introduction by Garrett Green, *On Religion: The Revelation of God as the Sublimation of Religion*, by Karl Barth (T&T Clark, 2006), pp. 1–29, and especially note 38, p. 130. Despite their significant point of agreement mentioned here, Green rightly states that Barth's use of the Hegelian term in writing of revelation as "the *Aufhebung* of religion" does not mean religion's "abolition," as initially translated,

but, more correctly, its "sublimation," in the sense of its being taken up and converted dialectically into a more adequate frame of reference. See also André Dumas, *Dietrich Bonhoeffer: Theologian of Reality* (Macmillan, 1968), pp. 178–184.

44. *Letters and Papers from Prison*, entry dated July 16, 1944, pp. 218.

45. See Toby Lester, "Oh, Gods!," *Atlantic Monthly*, February 2002, pp. 37–45. Reference here is to p. 38.

46. *Letters and Papers from Prison*, entry dated July 16, 1944, p. 220.

47. Dietrich Bonhoeffer, *Ethics*, p. 64.

48. *Ibid.*, p. 61.

49. *Ibid.*, p. 23.

50. *Ibid.*, p. 7.

51. Dietrich Bonhoeffer, "What is Meant by 'Telling The Truth'?," *Ethics* (Macmillan, 1955), pp. 326–334. German original, "Was Heisst: Die Wahrheit Sagen?," *Ethik* (Chr. Kaiser Verlag, 1949), pp. 385–395.

52. *Ethics*, p. 71.

53. "An ethic of disposition or intention (*Gesinnungsethik*) is just as superficial as an ethik of consequences," *Ethics*, p. 42. See James Burtness, *Shaping the Future: The Ethics of Dietrich Bonhoeffer* (Fortress, 1985), p. 16. As his title suggests, Burtness's stress upon "taking responsibility for" God's future fails to distinguish sufficiently between responsibility *for* and the ability-to-respond *to* what is currently taking place from heaven in Bonhoeffer's ethics. Note in this connection, though independent of Bonhoeffer's reflections, H. Richard Niebuhr's characteristic thesis: "At the critical junctures in the history of Israel and of the early Christian community the decisive question . . . raised was not 'What is the goal?' nor yet 'What is the law?' but 'What is happening?' and then 'What is the fitting response to what is happening?'" *The Responsible Self: An Essay in Christian Moral Philosophy* (Harper & Row, 1963), p. 67.

54. *Ethics*, p. 18.

55. *Ethics*, p. 22.

56. *NRS*, p. 185. [*GS*, I, p. 165.]

57. *The Cost of Discipleship*, 1937 (New York: Macmillan, 1963; London: SCM, 1963); *Life Together*, 1938 (New York: Harper & Row, 1954; London: SCM, 1954).

58. See *Ethics*, pp. 382–383. Here Bonhoeffer displays the influence of Karl Barth, and Barth, in turn, later refers to Bonhoeffer. From the index of references to Bonhoeffer in Barth's *Church Dogmatics*, see on this particular point of God's *commanding* as also the *permitting* and *granting* of the freedom of being responsible the comments in III, 4, pp. 14–15.

59. See André Dumas'critique, *Dietrich Bonhoeffer: Theologian of Reality*, pp. 215–235, and James Burtness's response, *Shaping the Future: The Ethics of Dietrich Bonhoeffer*, pp. 67–68.

60. *Ethics*, p. 372.

61. *Ethics*, p. 380.

62. *Letters and Papers from Prison*, p. 17.

63. Paul Lehmann, *The Decalogue and a Human Future* (Eerdmans, 1995) and *The Transfiguration of Politics* (Harper & Row, 1975). See also Nancy

J. Duff, *Humanization and the Politics of God: The* Koinonia *Ethics of Paul Lehmann* (Eerdmans, 1992), and the references to "responsibility" and "apocalyptic" in *Explorations in Christian Theology and Ethics: Essays in Conversation with Paul L. Lehmann,* edited by Philip G. Ziegler and Michelle J. Bartel (Ashgate, 2009).

64. Susan Owen, "Forgiveness and a Return to the Good," Ph.D. Dissertation, Department of Religious Studies, University of Virginia, August 1997, p. 19. Kantian scholars dispute the role of extra-human assistance in his moral thought. For a reading that sees Kant in *Religion within the Limits of Reason Alone* as closer to traditional Christianity in appealing to "heavenly influences" or "cooperation from above" and yet failing to show "*that* he can appeal to such assistance given the rest of his theory," see John E. Hare, *The Moral Gap: Kantian Ethics, Human Limits, and God's Assistance* (Clarendon Press, 1996), pp. 62, 67.

65. This is apparent in Elizabeth Anscombe's influential discussion of deontological and virtue ethics in which she claims that Christianity has a "law conception of ethics" stemming from the biblical Torah that [in her judgment, lamentably] was "substantially given up among Protestants at the time of the Reformation." The alternative she poses, and criticizes, is an utilitarian ethics of "consequentialism." But in none of the three, as contrasted, deontological, virtue, or consequentialist ethics, does news of heaven and how closely divine agency is associated with it in biblical apocalyptic play any part. See G.E.M. Anscombe's 1958 essay, "Modern Moral Philosophy," in *Virtue Ethics,* ed. Roger Crisp and Michael Slate (Oxford: 1997), pp. 26–44, quoted from pp. 30–31.

66. Alain Badiou, *Ethics: An Essay on the Understanding of Evil* (Verso, 2001), p. 47. For critical comment on Badiou's atheist rejection of an Aristotelian virtue ethics and a countering affirmation of a Thomistic ethics more in keeping with the direction of desire for *beatitude* or blessedness, the revised *eudaimonia* or well-being of Aristotle that Thomas attributes to the love of God, see Terry Eagleton, *Trouble With Strangers: A Study of Ethics* (Wiley-Blackwell, 2009), pp. 148, 269, and 307. Taking no account of the counter direction of the grace of Calvin's heavenly *virtus,* that arguably in some respects resonates more in Badiou's un-virtuous hearing of Paul's declaration of the Resurrection, Eagleton writes, "What the Aristotelians call virtue, or the spontaneous capacity for acting well, Christianity calls grace," p. 307.

67. Badiou, *Ethics,* pp. 122–124.

Chapter 5: The Hope of Heaven

1. Augustine, *The City of God, Basic Writings of Saint Augustine,* Vol. 2 (Random House, 1948), Book XXII, Chapter XXX, p. 663.

2. James A. Weisheipl, O.P., *Friar Thomas D'Aquino: His Life, Thought, and Works* (Doubleday: 1974; Catholic University of America Press: 1983), pp. 321–322.

3. Karl Barth, *Evangelical Theology* (Eerdmans, 1963), pp. 140–141.

4. Susan Howatch, *Glittering Images* (Fawcett Crest, 1987), p. 27.

5. In addition to numerous references in the Old Testament, see Mt. 1.20, 10.26, 10.28, 10.31, 14.27, 17.7, 28.10; Mk 5.36, 6.50; Lk. 1.13, 1.30, 2.10, 5.10, 8.50, 12.4, 12.7, 12.32; Jn 6.20, 12.15, 14.27; Acts 18.9; Rom. 8.15; 2 Tim. 1.7; Heb. 2.15; 1 Pet. 3.14; 1 Jn 4.18; and Rev. 1.17, 2.10.

6. John Leland, "Heaven Comes Down To Earth," *The New York Times Week in Review*, Section 4, p. 1., December 21, 2003.

7. Dion De Marbelle, "When They Ring the Golden Bells," 1887, *Best Revival Songs* (Cokesbury, 1924), p. 66.

8. Note again the titles listed in endnotes 6–9 of Chapter 1.

9. An email from James F. Kay, author of *Christus Praesens: A Reconsideration of Rudolf Bultmann's Christology* (Eerdmans, 1994), upon reading Anthony Everitt's *Cicero: The Life and Times of Rome's Greatest Politician* (Random House, 2003), referring to pages 182 and 257, where words from Cicero's *Tusculanae disputationes* XXX 74–31, 75 and *De Republica* VI 16 are quoted.

10. See in this connection, Alan F. Segal, *Life After Death: A History of the Afterlife in the Religions of the West* (Doubleday, 2004).

11. These words describing a vision of the heavenly Jerusalem are from Peter Abelard's (1079–1142) hymn, "O What Their Joy and Their Glory Must Be," as translated by John M. Neale (1818–1866), and found in various denominational hymnals.

12. John E. Thiel, "For What May We Hope? Thoughts on the Eschatological Imagination," *Theological Studies*, 67, 2006, pp. 517–541. In both an appeal to Karl Rahner, who "is certainly correct in his view that experience and talk of the *eschata* grow out of the present moment and 'only thus' may the *eschata* be represented theologically" as "the fulfillment of the human quest for God," and at the same time a critical revision of Rahner's lingering Kantianism that causes him to safeguard against speculative fantasies about the life of the blessed dead by enclosing them in a divine mystery that makes their state of blessedness in the afterlife "not capable of meaningful description," Thiel proposes imagining a continuation not only of Christ's reconciling ministry with the participation of the blessed in the afterlife, but a continuation as well of the blessed ones' discipleship in imitating the life proclaimed in the Gospel accounts of the Risen Christ's appearances.

13. Peter S. Hawkins, *Undiscovered Country: Imagining the World to Come* (Seabury, 2009), p. 83.

14. "O Happy Day, that Fixed My Choice," by Philip Doddridge, 1755. See, among many places, *The United Methodist Hymnal* (The United Methodist Publishing House, 1989), p. 391.

15. For a brief summary, see "Purgatory" in *The Oxford Encyclopedia of the Reformation*, Vol. 3, ed. Hans J. Hillerbrand (Oxford University Press, 1996), pp. 363–364.

16. See, as noted earlier, Christopher Morse, "Paul Lehmann as Nurturer of Theological Discernment," in *Explorations in Christian Theology and Ethics: Essays in Conversation with Paul L. Lehmann*, ed. Philip G. Ziegler and Michelle J. Bartel (Ashgate, 2009), pp. 11–28.

17. The lines are taken from William Butler Yeats, "The Second Coming,"

cited by Lehmann from *The Collected Poems of W. B. Yeats* (New York: The Macmillan Company, 1951), pp. 184–185, and quoted in his Preface to *The Transfiguration of Politics* (Harper & Row: 1975), p. xi.

18. Paul Lehmann, *Ethics in a Christian Context* (Westminster John Knox Press, 1963, 2006), p. 87.

19. See Morse, "Rachel's Refusal," in *Not Every Spirit: A Dogmatics of Christian Disbelief*, 2nd edn (T.& T. Clark, 2009), pp. 9–12.

20. Aristotle, *Politics*, Bk. 1, 1252a24-b15, 1259a38-60b26, and Chapters 3–7, translated by Trevor J. Saunders in *Aristotle: Politics, Books I and II* (Clarendon Press, 1995), pp. 2–21.

21. For how "the natural slave" ideology came to be justified theologically as either a "positive good" or a "necessary evil" in shaping American culture prior to the Civil War, see Larry E. Tise, *Proslavery: A History of the Defense of Slavery in America, 1701–1840* (The University of Georgia Press, 1987).

22. See Gregory of Nyssa's *Homilies IV*, referred to in Peter Garnsey, *Ideas of Slavery from Aristotle to Augustine* (Cambridge: 1996), pp. 80–85. Garnsey writes in his conclusion, "It will surprise no one that the hero of my narrative is Gregory of Nyssa who, perhaps uniquely, saw that slavery itself is a sin," p. 243.

23. See "St. Lazarus of Bethany," by Léon Clugnet, *The Catholic Encyclopedia* (Robert Appleton Company: 1910), http://www.newadvent.org/cathen/09097a.htm.

24. Of this plural and communal dimension of heaven's forthcoming, Robert Jenson writes: "Heaven is where God takes space in his creation to be present to the whole of it; he does that in the church," an apt statement as long as "the church" is understood to be those "called forth" from death to new life as Lazarus, unbounded by the grave clothes of any contrary type of ecclesiasticism. Robert W. Jenson, *Systematic Theology Vol. 1: The Triune God* (Oxford: 1997), p. 206. In this respect the medieval legends claiming that the raised Lazarus later became the first Bishop of Marseilles were at least right in their instinct to affirm such a life called forth by "the resurrection and the life" as ecclesial!

25. Johannes Weiss, *Jesus' Proclamation of the Kingdom of God* 1892 (Fortress, 1971), p. 136.

26. Johannes Weiss, JPKG, pp. 135–136.

27. Translated from the German by Theodore Baker, 1894, as "Lo, How a Rose E'er Blooming," published in a number of denominational hymnals, including *The United Methodist Hymnal* (The United Methodist Publishing House, 1989), p. 216.

28. See Alasdair MacIntyre's Giffert Lectures of 1988, *Three Rival Versions of Moral Enquiry: Encyclopaedia, Genealogy, and Tradition* (University of Notre Dame Press, 1990).

29. Martinus C. de Boer, "The Death of Jesus Christ and His Coming in the Flesh (1 Jn 4.2)," *Novum Testamentum* 33, October 1991, p. 345. For my further discussion of the dogmatic significance of these two terms see, *Not Every Spirit: A Dogmatics of Christian Disbelief*, 2nd edn (T&T Clark, 2009), pp. 38–40 and 354–355, where I suggest that "Paul's reference to 'in

NOTES TO PAGES 121–122 ❖ 141

the cross' is his nearest equivalent, *mutatis mutandis*, to the positive Johannine sense of 'in the flesh'." See Gal. 6.14.

30. *D. Martin Luther's Werke* (Weimar: Herman Böulau, 1901), 23.734. The terminological distinction is not to be taken as absolute, but applicable in specific contexts. More than twelve centuries earlier Ignatius of Antioch, in emphasizing Christ's saving enfleshment, uses *kata sarka* not with the sense Paul gives it in 2 Cor. 5.16 which Luther follows here, but with the same sense of *en sarki* as found in 1 John 4.2. He writes of Christ as "in truth of the family of David *kata sarka*" and "truly nailed *en sarki* under Pontius Pilate" in making the point that since Christ is "our true life" whoever does not confess that the Lord "was clothed in flesh" is "clothed with a corpse." See Ignatius, *Epistle to the Smyrnaeans*, Chs. 1, 4–5, *The Apostolic Fathers*, Vol. 1 (Harvard University Press, 1952), pp. 253–257.

31. Scholarly distinctions between so-called "realized, or inaugurated, eschatology" and "futurist, or transcendental, eschatology" have their place as textbook classifications, and various passages taken alone may reflect one or the other, but as the legacy of reflection responsive to Weiss's claims shows, as well as does Martha's and Mary's witness, the Gospel news itself resists accommodation to classifications drawn according to our time frames and stipulations. "But do not ignore this one fact, beloved," we hear from the Second Letter of Peter, "that with the Lord one day is like a thousand years, and a thousand years are like one day" (2 Pet. 3.8). And lest the univocal literalists without parabolic awareness and divinatory imagination try to use this equation to recalibrate their calculators in predicting the end times, the passage adds that this is not as "some think of slowness" (2 Peter: 3.9).

32. Romanus Cessario, O.P., *The Moral Virtues and Theological Ethics* (University of Notre Dame Press, 1991), p. 156.

INDEX OF BIBLICAL
REFERENCES

— ❖ —

INDEX OF NAMES

Bold page numbers indicate main passages.